Journey to Love is a book I didn't kı̇... robust understanding of love and what it truly means for love to be patient and kind. In our broken, racially fraught world, we all need to learn how to love better, deeper, richer. Matt's book shows us the way.

MICHELLE AMI REYES, vice president of Asian American Christian Collaborative, author of *Becoming All Things*

Gosh, this is a beautiful book. Matt's vivid stories and powerful insights will linger in your heart and mind long after you finish reading. When I was at one of the lowest times of my life, Matt reached out to show me love, so I know he practices what he preaches. Whether you come from a background where love was abundant or scarce, my prayer is that God will use Matt's words to open your heart to give—and receive—love.

DREW DYCK, editor, author of *Your Future Self Will Thank You*

In a world of power struggles and division, author Matt Mikalatos invites readers to do something extraordinary: inhale goodness and love *and* exhale it to those around them. *Journey to Love* is a rare opportunity, a respite for the weary soul, a breath of much-needed fresh air.

AUBREY SAMPSON, speaker, author of *Known*, *The Louder Song*, and *Overcomer*

I'm not sure how it's possible, but many of us manage somehow to take love for granted. With insight, honesty, and his trademark quick wit, Matt gently makes that impossible, by helping us see new depths in the oldest virtue. Any reader who goes on this *Journey to Love* will return changed, in the best and simplest of everyday ways.

PAUL J. PASTOR, author of *The Face of the Deep* and *The Listening Day*

This beautiful book of meditations inspired me to reflect on the ways I have been loved and how I can love others better. The author shares stories of how he learned what love is that are both personal and universal. In our heart of hearts, we all long to live a life of both receiving and giving love in deeper ways. This book identifies barriers to loving well and clearly defines what love is, so that we can live the life of love we are created to live.

JOYCE KOO DALRYMPLE, JD, pastor of discipleship at Wellspring Alliance Church

We all want to love and be loved. But what does that mean? Through winsome stories and heartfelt reflections, Matt Mikalatos gently probes what love looks like as he welcomes us on a life-changing journey. Don't miss not only reading this book but putting it into practice. You'll never be the same!

AMY BOUCHER PYE, author of *7 Ways to Pray*

Despite the Beatles' assurances that learning the game of love is easy, I've found we all struggle deeply with this basic need: to receive love, and to love well. In *Journey to Love*, Matt invites us to follow him into a life bursting with love. Our steps are small and halting at first. But as the journey progresses, we find ourselves running, then sprinting, and finally diving headlong into a mystery that's bigger and deeper than we imagined. *Journey to Love* is for anyone you know. Literally. Read it for yourself. Then read it with a friend. Or maybe someone who isn't a friend quite yet. This book is medicine for our hurting world.

JR. FORASTEROS, author of *Empathy for the Devil*

Journey to Love is simply beautiful. Personal and practical, Matt made me feel loved, made me want to love, and showed me how to love. The world will be a better, more loving place because of this book.

ANGIE WARD, PhD, assistant director of DMin at Denver Seminary, author of *I Am a Leader*

Journey to Love is a much-needed reminder that love is not only an emotion but a spiritual discipline and practice. Matt Mikalatos gives readers poignant stories to connect with our hearts and practical exercises inviting us to love with our whole selves. You'll want to read this book with a journal and practice it with a community.

KATHY KHANG, author of *Raise Your Voice* and cohost of *The Fascinating Podcast*

We spend years investing in education, professions, hobbies . . . but what about love? Do we give any thought toward growing in our ability to give and receive this most precious resource? A quick look at the world—or ourselves—shows how much we could use a journey to love, and in these forty easy-to-read reflections, author Matt Mikalatos gives us the nudge we need.

CATHERINE McNIEL, author of *All Shall Be Well* and *Long Days of Small Things*

Wherever you are on your own journey to love, you will find your next step in this book. Through thoughtful reflections and simple, practical exercises, Mikalatos encourages and challenges readers to act toward believing in and freely expressing radical love. In our divisive culture, this book is a refreshing call to a transformational way of living that is possible for any of us.

GINA BRENNA BUTZ, author of *Making Peace with Change*

Matt Mikalatos is a fair, wise, and trusted voice online and in person. His new book, *Journey to Love*, is exactly what our splintered, weary world needs. I especially appreciate the example of the beautiful, healthy, loving friendship Matt, a married man, shared with Shasta, a single woman. A gifted writer and communicator, Matt fills these pages with inspiring stories, hard-won lessons, and challenges to move us toward greater love. Thank you for pointing us back to what really matters.

VIVIAN MABUNI, national speaker, founder of *Someday Is Here* podcast, author of *Open Hands, Willing Heart*

There are highly regarded books that you slog through, wearily wondering what the fuss is about. And then there are books you didn't know you needed until the first chapter grabs you by the heart and doesn't let go. In *Journey to Love*, Matt Mikalatos serves as expert trail guide on a lyrical exploration of the most maligned, misunderstood, transformative power in the universe: love. Share this beautifully crafted love letter with everyone you know.

MAGGIE WALLEM ROWE, speaker, dramatist, author of *This Life We Share*

Journey to Love is an experience you don't want to miss. Each entry, reflection, and exercise will delve deep into your soul, cause you to ponder, and ultimately change your heart. Someone once said, "If we don't love, we will not live." Matt guides us on a journey, showing us how to give and receive love, how to delight in God's love, and ultimately how to live. I laughed (and yes, I cried) as I read of and embraced the tenderness and power of my Savior's love for me. Through Scripture, personal experiences, and practical applications, *Journey to Love* will change your life—it did mine.

DR. CYNTHIA FANTASIA, author of *In the Lingering Light*

Journey to Love is an invitation to peer into a truly vulnerable and sacred pilgrimage of love that author and sojourner Matt Mikalatos has committed his life to. With every shared story and soul-stirring perspective, you'll long to love more.

DESTINEE REA, cofounder of BOLD

Journey to Love gives attention to timeless secrets of a life well lived. We should never tire of our authors setting the table of love and grace before us. Every generation is hungry. I'm grateful Matt is doing his part, illuminating all sides of the heart and mind—and the world-changing subject of love.

CHARLIE PEACOCK, Grammy Award–winning music producer, author, founder of the commercial music program at Lipscomb University

journey to love

WHAT WE LONG FOR,
HOW TO FIND IT, AND
HOW TO PASS IT ON

MATT MIKALATOS

A NavPress resource published in alliance
with Tyndale House Publishers

NavPress is the publishing ministry of The Navigators, an international Christian organization and leader in personal spiritual development. NavPress is committed to helping people grow spiritually and enjoy lives of meaning and hope through personal and group resources that are biblically rooted, culturally relevant, and highly practical.

For more information, visit NavPress.com.

To my parents, Pete and Maggie Mikalatos, who loved me first and gave me a long, long head start on the journey to love. I am deeply thankful to you both and love you a lot.

CONTENTS

The greatest thing you'll ever learn
is just to love and be loved in return.
eden ahbez

INTRODUCTION

$\mathcal{B}$efore she died, my friend Shasta asked me if I would speak at her funeral.

She sounded uncertain, even a little awkward when she asked, like maybe I would say no. Which seemed ridiculous, laughable even, after all we had been through the last four years. The cancer diagnosis, the surgery, the chemo, the radiation, her hair falling out, the painful side effects from the treatment, the giddy moments when the doctor said it was all working, the sobbing disappointment when it wasn't. I had driven her to countless doctor's appointments, filled out financial paperwork, done her laundry, washed the dishes, cooked meals, bought groceries, and a hundred other things.

I had been dreading her question, had been trying to avoid it. I kept holding on to hope, kept suggesting that there would be a new treatment, a new doctor, a healing, something. I kept saying we didn't know what was going to happen. I was still trying to convince myself that death—her death, at least, her imminent death—wasn't a sure thing. We didn't need to make these sorts of plans.

But today I was sitting on the floor beside her bed, like I had done so many times before, and she was lying there, her face toward me. The sunlight from her window shone on her scalp, her hair gone again in a last-ditch effort to slow the gnawing sickness that was eating her lungs, her liver, her breasts, her bones. She was too thin. And she was too tired for me to keep sidestepping this conversation.

For four years, I had worked to make sure that when she asked me for something, the answer was always yes. But this question . . . I wasn't sure if I could do it. Because she had said, "*When* I die" instead of "*If* I die," and everything in me wanted to say to her, "We just don't know what's going to happen. You could live another twenty years. You could outlive us all. You might have to speak at *my* funeral."

But instead I said, "Of course," and we both burst into tears.

Not fighting that "when" felt like the first step off a cliff. We were in free fall now, and there was no more denying that gravity had taken control.

We were both still crying when I managed to choke out the words, "What do you want me to say?"

A new strength seemed to come over her. Her tears stopped, and there was a determination in her eyes. She didn't need to think for a moment about my question.

"I want you to tell them that they are loved," she said.

"Who?" I asked.

So she gave me a list. Her parents. Her brother. Her niece and nephew, her sister-in-law, all her family. Her friends. Those who had stuck by her to the end, those who had quietly disappeared as she sank into deeper illness, those who hadn't spoken to her in years, those who had betrayed and hurt her. The friends of her parents who would come to show their support. The strangers. The church staff at her funeral.

This desire of hers to tell people they were loved did not come as a surprise. Shasta was the woman who knew the name of every employee at the local pho shop and the names of their family still in Vietnam. She had befriended the checker at the local grocery store and been to see his jazz band play on a Friday night. She counseled the nurses about their personal lives while she sat in the wide chair, chemicals dripping into her veins.

"Everyone," she said at last. "I want you to tell everyone how much they are loved."

I thought of the vast number of people in the world. Of the people who know love well, who have lived with it their whole lives. Of the people who have never been loved, who scarcely believe it exists. Of those who are like broken cups, who feel any love that comes to them just seems to drain away through some unseen crack, some hole in their hearts.

I thought of the many times when I had been unsure I was loved, the astonishing loneliness of that question. I thought of the times love had filled me like helium, when I thought I might lift off the ground from the joy of it all. I thought of my dear friend. For the last year, we had never let a day go by without telling each other, "I love you." A text, a phone call, face-to-face—we hadn't missed a day. Now she was asking me for a miracle. Tell everyone, every person I could find, that they are loved. I didn't see how I could do it. On the other hand, I didn't see how I could say no. Not to her.

"Okay," I said. "Okay."

She smiled, radiant with affection, and said, "I knew you would say yes." She closed her eyes, still smiling. I wiped the last tear from her face. I pulled her blanket over her shoulders, and a gentle peace seemed to cover her too. She hadn't said, "Write a love letter to every person on the planet," but she knew me. She knew that's what I would do.

She knew that I would be turning it over in my mind—how to take you on a journey to love. How to show you the sights, how to lay out the map, how to walk with you from here to there.

So here it is. My best attempt at keeping my promise. Let's take this journey together, and trust that if our paths are different, we are still headed to the same destination. *You are loved.* My hope is that we can move past hearing those words and get to the place where we truly, honestly experience it, believe it, and can show others that it is true of them as well.

PART ONE

Preparing for the Journey

Describing love is like describing
the mountain on which you are standing.

You want to tell of snow-capped peaks,
the sun splashed on wide swaths of stone.
You want to say, "See how it towers over the valley.
See how its long shadow covers the world!"

But where you stand, you only see a meadow
bursting with orange flowers and the deer
walking single file, their ears flicking
toward the song of water over smooth stones.

Love is like that.

You want to say it changes everything,
say every person on earth is painted with it,
say it is the towering truth of the world,
say that it conquers, captures, collides with us all.

But what you see is a kitchen when you are six.
Your father lifts you to the counter
and spreads strawberry jam on toast
and you didn't even know in that moment

that this was love because you asked for bread
and your father gave you toast
and not a stone.

1

LOVE EXISTS

Three things will last forever—faith, hope, and love—and the greatest of these is love.[1]

ST. PAUL

About six months after Shasta passed away, I made a new friend. This was a big deal. I was still raw emotionally, still recovering, still struggling to sleep through the night, and really just sticking to relationships that felt easier to carry— my wife, my kids, my family and closest friends. But I met Quentin, and I really liked the guy. I made some effort to build a friendship. We grabbed lunch from time to time, and we enjoyed hanging out.

Quentin was going through some hard times—a water leak in his apartment had ruined all his belongings, and then he found out there was asbestos in it. Then, to make matters worse, he texted me a picture of his lungs from a doctor's appointment. He had lung damage from the asbestos. He was going to need to raise some money to get a hotel room, replace his belongings, and now have surgery.

I kept staring at that picture. Shasta's breast cancer had spread into her lungs, and I had seen plenty of scans. And Quentin's "asbestos damage" looked suspiciously like cancer to me. I sent the picture to my doctor friend, who told me that the scan was of advanced cancer in the lungs. Furious, I pushed on some other details. That's when I discovered that Quentin was a con artist. There was no leak in his apartment. His belongings weren't damaged. He hadn't been exposed to asbestos. He was befriending me to use me, to get my money. And, worse, knowing what had happened to my good friend, he had *sent me a picture of lung cancer.*

Have you found yourself in a moment like that? Where you thought someone was your friend, only to discover they were just trying to get something from you, to use you? And it's no surprise—in fact, it's to be expected— that you would walk away from an experience like that and have your doubts about the existence of true friendship, of real affection, of love.

One of our first fears about the journey to love can be *What if no one ever really loves me? What if the whole thing is a myth or a fantasy? What if other people are pretending? What if I've fooled myself into believing that it's something I can find, and it just . . . isn't?*

These are frightening and painful questions. Many of us have asked whether our parents truly love us. Some of us have wondered that about a spouse or partner, or even asked whether there's anyone out there who would want to be in relationship with us at all.

But if love isn't real, then we have universally—as human beings—fooled ourselves.

Love is a concept that every people group on earth believes in. Some languages make no distinction between the colors green and blue.[2] At least one language doesn't have numbers.[3] There are words that appear in one language but not in others. But every language in the world, without exception, has a word for love. Love is a universal human concept.

The most ancient human literature talks about love of some kind, going back to when we first started recording our stories, poems, and thoughts in written form:

- Almost five thousand years ago, a Sumerian king named Shuruppak wrote to his son that "a loving heart maintains a family."[4]
- Our oldest versions of *The Epic of Gilgamesh* are four thousand years old, and in it, our hero Gilgamesh speaks of his love for his dear friend Enkidu.
- Almost three thousand years ago, the Chinese poet Meng Jiao wrote a poem about the love of a mother for her child in "A Traveler's Song."
- There is some debate over the date, but at least 2,400 years ago, the Hebrew book of Job—one of the oldest complete works of human literature—tells the story of a man who loses everything, even though he is a good person. He speaks of receiving love from God

when he says, "You have granted me life and steadfast love, and your care has preserved my spirit."[5]

Four thousand years ago, people were thinking about love. Four thousand years from now, people will still be thinking about love, talking about love, trying to understand love.

So here we are. I know you're wanting to talk about love, to grow in love, to become more loving, or you wouldn't be reading this book. Maybe, like me, you're dealing with an endless well of grief or sorrow and not sure how you could possibly add another relationship, or how to handle the ones you have. Maybe you're tired, or broken, or numb. Maybe you've been hurt, and your heart gives you a sharp warning every time you think about trusting someone else. Maybe you've reached a plateau, and you see the mountain of love rising over you, and you're saying to yourself, *Where I am is good, but I want to go higher.*

However you're feeling, most of us have so many questions as we set out on this journey:

- ▸ What is love?
- ▸ How do I find it?
- ▸ How do I learn to accept love?
- ▸ How can I learn to love other people?
- ▸ If love exists, what does that mean for me?
- ▸ Why haven't I experienced love?

We need to explore all these excellent questions. But there is one we can lay to rest: Does love exist? We already know the answer.

Love is. Love was. Love will be.

REFLECTION

Are you ready for the journey ahead? How are you feeling? Excited? Scared? Tired? Angry? What are you hoping for as we move together on this journey?

EXERCISE

Describe the state of your life as if it were a house. What does it look like? What condition is it in? What do you like about it, and what do you want to change? Write this description down, or draw a picture, or record a video about it, so you can remember this in the future. If you're feeling brave, share it with someone.

2

IT'S NOT YOU

Love isn't a state of perfect caring. It is an active noun like
struggle. To love someone is to strive to accept that person
exactly the way he or she is, right here and now.

FRED ROGERS

When my face went numb, I finally agreed to go to the emergency room.

Soon I was renting a pricey ER room and lounging in a robe that opened in the back while nurses attached wires and drew blood. They did an EKG. They wheeled me down the hallway to get an X-ray. They took my blood pressure.

Two hours later, the doctor said, "It's not your heart."

EKGs, X-rays, and a troponin test all said the same thing: Whatever was wrong, it wasn't my heart. In fact, my doctor said, "All the tests show the results we would expect from a healthy young man."

I told her I knew she was exaggerating because I wasn't particularly young, and she laughed and said, "Matt, the troponin test tells me that not only are you not having a heart attack, but you haven't had one in the last several days, and you're not even thinking about having one tonight."

I was skeptical. I told her my symptoms again.

She told me again, "Whatever is wrong, it's not your heart."

I pointed out that my left arm was hurting. The chest pains. My face was numb—had I mentioned that?

"It's not your heart," she said, firmly. "Go home."

Sometimes we know something is wrong, and we fixate on finding a reason for it. And we're pretty good at coming up with an answer that matches most or all of the symptoms. We can do this with interpersonal problems, or with physical issues like chest pain, or even when we're looking at love—or the lack of it—in our own lives.

When it comes to love, we look at what seems to be broken—where love seems to be missing or unhealthy or unkind—and we add them all up like a math problem. We ask questions like, *Why don't I have more friends?* or *Why don't more people love me?*

The symptoms vary from person to person. An inability to find a spouse, or to stay in a long-term relationship. Terrible family history. Broken relationships. People who should be loving (a parent, maybe) but are abusive and cruel. *Why does it seem like all the people around me secretly dislike me?*

Most of us come to a singular conclusion—one that is backed up by romantic comedies and people on the internet and the misguided wisdom of "common knowledge": *If you don't have love in your life, something is wrong with you.*

Now it's my job to run all the tests and write on my chart and give you the verdict:

- ▸ It's not you.
- ▸ You're not the reason.

Worse people than you have been loved. People more broken than you have been loved. People who are more cruel, less intelligent, more antisocial, less committed to finding love have been loved.

It's not your heart, your personality, the way you look, or even the way you act.

That's not the reason you're lacking love in your life.

You probably want to argue against that. You want to tell me all your symptoms. You want me to know there's something broken in the core of you that keeps love away.

To which I can only reply, "It's not your heart."

I'm not saying you don't have room to grow. Who doesn't? You certainly may be avoiding love, pushing it away, sabotaging it, spitting on it, dodging it.

But it's not your heart preventing you from being loved.

It's not your heart preventing you from loving.

The reason you're struggling with love?

It's not you.

Love is available to you. Love is accessible. You are not fundamentally separated from love.

It's not your heart.

Let's start with that.

REFLECTION

What is your internal reaction to the statement that "it's not your heart"? How do you feel when you're told that whatever is causing you to be missing love in your life, it's not because of who you are? Do you find that easy to believe, or difficult? If it is true, what would that mean for your life?

EXERCISE

Take a piece of paper and write "Ten reasons I am worthy of love" at the top. If you get stuck, put the paper somewhere prominent. Every time you pass it, try to add one thing to the list.

3

WHAT LIES AHEAD

Our real journey in life is interior; it is a matter of growth, deepening, and of an ever greater surrender to the creative action of love and grace in our hearts.

THOMAS MERTON

*M*y wife, Krista, wants to walk the Camino de Santiago someday. It's a Catholic pilgrimage that runs in a network of paths toward the cathedral of Santiago de Compostela in northwestern Spain. People have been walking these paths since the Middle Ages. It's a journey that begins at home, wherever that may be, and ends in the resting place, so we are told, of St. James, one of the earliest followers of Jesus.

My wife isn't Catholic, though.

In fact, the many people who walk the Camino (over 300,000 annually, in recent years) are of varying faiths, ages, genders, backgrounds, nationalities, cultures, and philosophies. They each have their own deeply personal reasons for the journey ahead of them.

Krista would like to go, I think, to bond with her friends who would join her, and because she loves hiking and international living, and of course in the hope that the journey would have a spiritual benefit. But there are others on the Camino just looking to get in shape, or to say they have done it, or to honor a loved one who can't make the walk themselves, or because they love history, or even to write a travel book.

The journey to love is like this too.

We can't make assumptions about the other people on the road—where they've come from, what they're looking for, the struggles they're facing along the way. They may have different motives than ours, and they may be moving at a different speed along the path. Perhaps they are alone—maybe they have always been alone—or maybe they are in a tight-knit group and are unlikely to befriend others along the way.

There are people of all kinds walking the path beside us, from other cultures and traditions and religions.

There are people who are intensely serious about it, and well prepared: They've bought the no-rub socks and sturdy shoes and a lightweight pack and plenty of water. They've read every book about love, watched every movie, plotted and planned and prepared for this next step.

And there are tourists who seem to have wandered onto the path today in flip-flops, carrying a bottle of sunscreen, looking around and saying, "Oh, isn't that nice!" and taking photos. There are people who wander into the journey who aren't planning for the long haul, who are more in love with the idea of love—*Here's me standing in front of the cathedral!*—than they are about any true transformative experience.

Another thing about the journey to love is that, just like on the Camino de Santiago, we all start from different paths. Some walked a thousand miles to get to where they are, and some walked a hundred. Some were dropped off in cars or took the journey by bicycle. Some were even born in the town where the cathedral has sat for hundreds of years. For them, the journey is no trek; it's the church they've walked past on their way to the grocery.

For instance, I grew up in a loving home with two parents who cared deeply for me and my siblings. I never had to question if they loved me because they told me literally every day—often multiple times a day. That gives me a pretty big leap ahead in my journey. For someone whose parents neglected them or abused them or simply weren't demonstrative with love, or whose parents were absent—even out of necessity—or perhaps just didn't know how to express their true, deep love for their children, there's a longer trek to be taken. They have unanswered questions, and lessons to be learned that may have come easily and at a young age in some other family.

It's tempting sometimes to compare our journeys. We may feel bitterness toward those who have been born into the city of Love, when we had to fly and drive and hike our way in. Or those who had short journeys may not understand the true difficulties of those who have come from farther away. And, too, some of us may have lived in that fine city once upon a time, but now we find ourselves in exile, alone, uncertain how to return.

As we prepare for the journey ahead, it's important that we not compare our journey to that of those around us. We need to focus on our own path, our own steps toward love. If we have been wronged in our journey thus far, so be it. That can't be changed by comparing ourselves to someone who had it easier. The question is not where I have been, or where others have been, but *Where am I now?* and *Where do I want to end up?* and *What will I need for this journey?* Let's prepare for what lies ahead.

REFLECTION

Consider your journey and the path ahead: Where am I now in relation to love? Where do I want to be? What do I need for that journey?

EXERCISE

Write the word *love* in the middle of a blank page. Then draw the journey to love you have taken so far in your life—the ins and outs, your visits or near visits, the terrain you walked through, and where you are today.

4

ALL YOU HAVE TO DO
IS SHOW UP

I am poor and naked, but I am the chief of the nation. We do not
want riches but we do want to train our children right. Riches
would do us no good. We could not take them with us to the
other world. We do not want riches. We want peace and love.

RED CLOUD

A few years ago, a pastor named JR. Forasteros invited
me to come speak at his church. He had read a couple of my
books. He had reviewed one for a magazine. He friended me
online, sent me the occasional note. Now he was flying me
out to Ohio. He wasn't going to put me up in a hotel. I was
going to stay with him and his wife, Amanda, at their place.

Another guy I knew only from brief online interactions—named Clay Morgan—was also planning to come.
He said he wanted to get to know me, so he was going to
stay with JR. too, and we'd all hang out.

The whole thing was a little weird. I didn't feel unsafe,
but I definitely thought, *Worst-case scenario, we're only talking*
about a couple of days.

During that weekend, these two guys kept making overtures of friendship. We went to the movies. We talked about life, and they shared deep things. They kept saying nice things about my writing. We talked about shared interests: monsters and movies and novels and a bunch of other things.

JR. had this booming laugh and a giant beard and a deep mind full of interesting insights. Clay was this tall, handsome man who had a way of making everyone into a friend after brief interactions. They were both kind. They were both friendly. And Amanda, JR.'s wife, was delightful.

It turned into a nice weekend. And it could have just been that, a brief engagement that turned into a sort of acquaintance with one another—the kind of relationship where we'd grab coffee if we ever managed to be in the same town.

But before I left, Clay said he had an amazing time and wondered aloud if the three of us should start talking more regularly. Maybe once a week?

And sure, I had enjoyed the weekend. But my life was full, and the thought of carving out an hour of my week for these guys . . . it didn't seem like a great investment of my time. I travel a lot. I spend a lot of weekends with strangers. I can't set aside an hour of my life for each one.

I told them I wasn't sure I had capacity for that with everything else going on in life. Scheduling time, finding a way to do it, all that stuff.

Then Clay said he and JR. would take care of the logistics. "All you'd have to do is show up," Clay said.

I wavered.

But then I said yes.

In the years to come, these two guys became my close friends. It's hard as adults to make new, deep friendships, but these are guys I hear from most every week, and they know my life and my family. They've spoken hard truths to me about myself and heard them about themselves.

It has been work. Hard work, sometimes.

But guess who I call when the worst things happen in my life?

Love comes to us in many different ways. It's not all spouses and parents and children. It's friends in unexpected places, the neighbor who ends up becoming a part of your family. The stranger who reaches out and offers friendship.

It takes time. Attention. Emotional energy. More than we might be willing to give. But most of us would say, "I want more love in my life." Are we ready to show up for it?

REFLECTION
"All you'd have to do is show up." That's what Clay said to me. Are there people in your life who have been reaching out to you? What have they been saying to you? What have you been saying to them?

EXERCISE
Think of a person you would like to get to know better as a friend, and invite them to do something fun this

week. A movie. Game night. A walk. Remember, this is an *invitation*. Don't take it too hard if they have other plans or turn you down. Extending an invitation prepares you to receive more love in your life, regardless of the answer.

5

PERMANENT RELATIONSHIP

Your task is not to seek for love, but merely to seek and find all the barriers within yourself that you have built against it.

RUMI

$\mathcal{M}$y wife, Krista, met Shasta in college. We have a picture of the two of them wading through a river. They're wearing shorts, and flannel shirts thrown over T-shirts, and they have that open-mouthed, hands-thrown-in-the-air look of people who are gingerly stepping through freezing water.

I met Shasta the summer Krista and I got married. She flew in to hang out with us, and we went to the beach in Northern California. Shasta went swimming there, telling everyone else to join her as she jumped, fully clothed, into the frigid surf. She was funny, and full of life, and had a way of looking at people with her full attention.

We crossed paths occasionally over the years, and eventually she started coming over to our house and playing with the kids. She took my kids and my nephew down to an empty parking lot and taught them to drive. (She grew up on a farm and felt that even nine-year-olds need some experience behind the wheel.) Our kids thought of her as part of the clan, like an aunt, maybe.

When she needed a break from her living situation, she'd come to stay at our house for a few nights. We gave her a key, so she could come any time she wanted. She'd sit out on our back porch in the mornings and drink her coffee and watch the sun rising and the birds flitting around the yard. She became entwined into our family. She came over for holidays. She joined us and our parents on vacations.

One day after Shasta was diagnosed, she told me it was okay if I needed to go away. There were other people in her life who needed some space during her illness. They couldn't handle it. She was understanding of that, and she loved our family, and she said, "I know this is hard. If it's too hard, that's okay." She was giving us an out, which I think is a sign of how much she loved us. She was willing to spare us pain by taking more on herself.

I said, "You keep saying that it's okay if we walk away from you. I want you to understand that we are in a permanent relationship. I'm not going away. I'm not leaving you. You don't have to give us an out. You don't have to ask yourself if we'll be with you. We're here to stay."

We'd had this conversation a few times . . . I think because Shasta knew how hard it was and because she was afraid we might drift away. Other friends had done that.

But somehow those two words stuck this time: permanent relationship.

It's the sort of thing you say to a sibling or one of your children, a family member. Shasta was already so close with our family, but those two words brought a peace. Whatever was to come, we weren't leaving this relationship. Not willingly.

It sounds wonderful, right? A deep, permanent relationship. A friendship that transcends labels and becomes something unquantifiable.

How did we get there? One step at a time, taking the journey over the course of years, until we reached, together, a place of affection that was more family than friends.

You may feel like your relationships are transient, that love flits in and out of your life, that permanence is an illusion. But I promise you, on this journey to love, if you're willing to put in the time and work, you can find these places of permanent relationship. Because that's just how love works.

It is hard work. It takes a lot of time.

But it's worth it.

The journey to love is always worth it.

REFLECTION

For many of us, the idea of sharing our true self with someone else makes us nervous, afraid, and uncertain. Do you find it easy or difficult to do that? What do you think would happen if you shared your deepest self with your friends?

EXERCISE

Make a list of all the "permanent relationships" you have. Is the list short or long? Are there other people you wish you could add to it? Are there people you are uncertain return the sentiment? What do you want to do about it?

PART TWO

Finding Love

"I want to find love."
Those were the five words
she said to the guru.
He rummaged around his hut
for the longest time,
then turned back to her
with an apologetic half shrug
to say, It's not here.
He smiled and asked her,
"Where did you see it last?"

6

RECOGNIZING LOVE

Love can only be found through the act of loving.
PAULO COELHO

"Do you think my father loved me?"

A few years ago, I wrote a book about fathers and daughters called *Sky Lantern*. As a result, every few months, I get an email from a father asking about reconnecting with his daughter, or a daughter asking if her dad really loved her.

This particular email was hard. Her father had passed away, and all her memories of him had to do with him critiquing her. He didn't celebrate her high school graduation, when she had been top of the class. He just asked her if she thought she could do it again in college. When she graduated college, he said it wasn't much compared to a master's degree. When she got her master's, he sighed and said maybe there would be something to celebrate if she managed to get her doctorate. He had died soon after. So, she was wondering, did he ever really love her?

We wrote back and forth for several weeks, and in each email, she revealed a little bit more. She argued both sides, like she was both the defense and the prosecution. *He said I was never good enough. But on the other hand, he paid for all my schooling. He never told me he was proud of me. But he told a lot of other people he was proud of me. He only told me that he loved me one single time. Still, there was that once . . .*

I asked the occasional question, and each one set her off on another series of arguments and counterarguments. I couldn't help but see a little bit of myself in the conversation as it twisted back and forth. We all have people who love us, or who should love us, theoretically. But even the most loving person has moments when they act in ways that don't seem loving. And sometimes someone who doesn't truly love us has a moment when they do something that appears loving, either by accident or to manipulate us. So how can we know if someone loves us or doesn't? And, maybe harder . . . how can we know when we truly love someone else? Because there are times when convenience, or habit, or expectation, or guilt causes us to act as if we love someone when maybe we don't.

The best we can do in moments of uncertainty is to be reminded of what love truly is, and what love isn't.

So I started saying to my new friend: Okay, love is gentle. Was your dad gentle with you? Okay, love is kind. Was your father kind? Love forgives. Love is patient.

She started adding it all up, doing the math. She came to a place where she said, "You know what? My dad had all the signs of loving me. Every time you say, 'Love is like this,' I look and see it in how he treated me. In fact, I look at how I show love to my son now, and a lot of it . . . a lot of it is the same, even though I can also tell him I love him. My dad was a complex man who never shared his emotions well. I think he loved me but he didn't know how to say it."

You know what?

I looked back over her many emails and stories of her father. And I think she was absolutely right.

REFLECTION

Imagine someone came to you confused about love— what it is, what it looks like, what its characteristics are. How would you describe love to them? What story would you tell? What words would you use?

EXERCISE

Ask a friend to tell you a story of one person whom they have no doubt loves them. What makes them so sure? When did they first realize this person loved them? What moments, actions, or words contribute to their confidence in this person's love?

7

GENTLENESS

I learned that it is the weak who are cruel, and that
gentleness is to be expected only from the strong.
LEO ROSTEN

We have frogs in our backyard, and when my daughters were small, they loved to catch them and hold them in their cupped hands. I'd always shout to them, "Be gentle!" It's children we're most likely to say this to, whether they're holding a living creature, interacting with other kids, or holding a treasured family heirloom.

That's the heart of gentleness, isn't it? Being aware of both your own strength and the fragility of the world around you. Gentleness is learning how not to hurt others. Gentleness is learning not to break things because you have misjudged your own strength or the sturdiness of someone or something around you.

Gentleness requires awareness of both myself (*How strong*

am I? How much power do I have?) and the people and world around me (*How fragile or easily broken are they?*).

For me, I find it easiest to lose my gentle spirit when interacting with my family. There are repeated tiny things that I find it simple to become angry over: Why does no one close the tortilla-chip bag? Why am I expected to do everyone's dishes? My response may be stronger than such little annoyances warrant and can do lasting hurt to someone's feelings.

Gentleness, then, is about power in reserve. I have strength, and rights, and privileges, and they are mine to use. They remain mine whether I exercise them or hold them in reserve. I don't have to use my entire strength. I don't have to demand my every right. I don't need to use my privilege only for myself.

Cultivating gentleness requires a greater awareness of people around me and a more honest awareness of myself. In fact, I've found that one of the best ways to practice gentleness is to make sure I am being gentle with myself. Like it or not, it is easier to be aware of others if I am doing the work to make sure I am healthy and well: well-rested, well-slept, well-exercised, taking care of my mental health, being mindful of my emotions.

And is gentleness an attribute of love? Absolutely. Search your memory for someone who was unfailingly gentle with you, someone who worked hard never to purposely harm you, and I guarantee you will find someone who loved you. Gentleness is hard work, and it is a gift to those we love.

There are complexities to be aware of. A parent has more power than a child in a relationship and can hurt them more easily. Complexities in the past of our relationships can create strange power dynamics that shift depending on the situation. My personal issues might make me more vulnerable than someone else. And on the front end of a new relationship, we often don't know one another's strengths and vulnerabilities very well yet.

Growing in our gentleness takes time and truthfulness . . . and a real curiosity about how our loved ones are doing, as well as how our words and actions are impacting people. It's a strange paradox that sometimes to grow in gentleness, I have to be mentally and emotionally tough—able to handle the truth about how I am interacting with people around me.

Gentleness requires us to stop and be aware of our own strength and the complicated vulnerabilities of the world around us. You are stronger than you think, and the world is more fragile than you might suspect.

REFLECTION
Think back on a time when someone you are close to unintentionally hurt your feelings. Would gentleness have changed the situation? Now think on a time when you unintentionally hurt someone else. Would being more aware of their sensitivity have helped you avoid it? Or being more aware of your own strength and power?

EXERCISE

Work hard today to exercise gentleness. Use less strength than you think you need in conversations and situations around you. If that's not enough, then carefully (gently) apply more. Pay attention to the power of your words and actions. Pay attention to the emotional state of people around you.

8

KINDNESS

Three things in human life are important. The first is to be kind. The second is to be kind. And the third is to be kind.

HENRY JAMES

Krista and I have three daughters, and we love them all deeply. There's a seven-year gap between our second and third kids, and that's largely because we had a few miscarriages. If you've not been through the miscarriage of a child you hoped for, it's a devastating thing. I was surprised by how deep the emotions are. You've started making plans for this big change—maybe painted the nursery or bought a stroller, picked out some clothes or a name—and after the miscarriage, all these things are just reminders of your loss.

During one of those miscarriages, we were in the hospital, talking to the doctor, and she was telling us what had happened. We were devastated. We texted a few close friends and family. My parents had the older girls, and we returned home to our house, feeling sad and low.

We walked into the house to discover it had been cleaned, top to bottom. The kitchen was spotless, the living room vacuumed. Things had been put away, straightened up, washed, polished.

When Shasta had learned about the miscarriage, she had used her key, let herself in, and cleaned the house. It didn't make our grief disappear, of course. But it was a relief, and a symbol of her love for our family, and we were so moved by it.

It was a *kindness*.

The words *kindness* and *kin* in English are related. Kin are family, people we are related to, which means kindness is a kind of adoption, in the best possible sense. Kindness is treating people who are not family as if they are. Whether it's for an afternoon, a brief moment at the grocery store, or something that's extended to our permanent relationships, kindness is bringing someone into the inner circle of your life. Kindness and love are linked because kindness is about family.

If I saw my sister's car broken down on the side of the road, I would stop and check on her and make sure she had what she needed, even if there was something else pressing in my schedule at the same time. With my family, I don't think of that as kindness (even though it is); it's just what you do for a sibling. But when I extend that family action to someone else, kindness is more easily recognized. Kindness is active, choosing to lay aside our own comforts to take care of someone else. A few years ago, one of our neighbors who we didn't know very well died. I spent an afternoon in the house cleaning and taking out the trash before her adult kids got home. That was kindness. And, of course, I've been the beneficiary of kindness many, many times in my life. When both of our cars broke down and we had no money, friends and family gifted money to us so we could buy a car, and another friend gave his car to us, no strings attached.

When my youngest daughter, Myca, was nine years old, she walked up to me and said, "We're all related."

I asked her, "What do you mean?"

"I was thinking about the story of Adam and Eve," she said. "They had kids, and their kids had kids, and then one day it came to us. So we're all related. Everybody is related to Adam and Eve."

"So what does that mean?"

Myca said, "We're all brothers and sisters. Or cousins. Related. So we should treat each other like family and be nice to everyone and love everyone."

"But what if someone is really different from me?"

"No matter what someone looks like or what they say or if they're mean to you, they're still family."

Myca has a very kind heart. And more than once, we've passed a homeless person asking for money at an exit ramp and she has burst into tears and said, "Why does the world have to be like this?" So we started carrying little packages with water and snacks and sewing kits to hand out to people like that when we cross their paths. Myca's kind heart won't allow us to do otherwise.

REFLECTION
Think back on three times you received kindness from others. And then think of three times you shared kindness with someone else.

EXERCISE
Plan an act of kindness. Kindness can be "in the moment," but it can also be planned. What's something you can do or say for someone in your neighborhood, or at your work, or at your place of worship, that would be an act of kindness? Make a plan, set a time, and do it!

9

PATIENCE

Patience . . . means to look at the thorn and see the
rose, to look at the night and see the dawn.

ELIF SHAFAK

*M*y parents put up with a lot from me when I was a kid.
I fought with my sisters (I'm honestly embarrassed looking
back at some of the ways I treated them), talked back about
various things, failed math class because I couldn't be bothered with the homework, more or less ditched home when I
got a girlfriend, and so on. Somehow, through all of it, they
were patient with me. And their *perspective* had a lot to do
with that.

How did perspective play a part? Well, my parents had
to keep reminding themselves, *This, too, shall pass.* Fourteen-
year-old boys grow up to become forty-year-old men, and at
least some maturity happens over that time. It takes patience
to believe that.

Patience says, *This person I love is growing and changing, and in time this will bring beauty in places that are not beautiful now. I can love this person for who they are today because I can see who they are becoming.*

Patience knows that love is not the work of a moment, but of a lifetime.

The patience we have is all about the perspective we choose. A friend of mine told me that she used to get angry with her kids, who, instead of putting their cereal bowls in the dishwasher, would fill them with water and put them in the sink, leaving her to empty them and load them in the dishwasher. She caught herself thinking, *It would only take them five seconds to put this dish away, and is that really so hard?*

But then she realized, *Oh, it only takes me five seconds to put it away, also, and it is making me angry for hours.* That perspective change helped her be patient with her kids. Does that mean she didn't tell them to put their dishes away anymore? Of course not. But when her kids failed, she was able to say, "In the grand scheme of things, this is a small issue." She prioritized relationship and chose to focus on her love for them over what bothered her.

Krista and I have found the same to be true with our kids. Sure, we have frustrations, but when we start comparing what's maddening against what's wonderful about our kids—their kind hearts, their focus on people around them, their love for one another—those little things, in perspective, seem less important. We believe that someday those kindhearted little creatures will pick up their socks in the living room.

Perspective creates space for patience, and patience itself is a kind of love. When we love through patience, we see not just who another is, but who they are becoming, and then—this is important—trust that change is coming rather than forcing them toward change.

Love makes patience possible because we're not going anywhere. We're in this relationship for the long haul. We embrace our loved ones for who they are today, not who we want them to be.

REFLECTION

When we're impatient with people we love, it's often because we're focused on who we want them to be rather than on who they are. Who has shown patience to you in the past? How did that make you feel? Whom are you struggling to be patient with in your life today?

EXERCISE

Think about the person you are struggling to be patient with. Set aside that impatience for a few minutes, and make a short list of things you appreciate about who that person is *today*. For bonus points: Send a text, write a note, or spend a few moments telling that person, "Here are some things I like about you."

10

FORGIVENESS

If someone wrongs you seven times in a day,
and they keep coming back and saying,
"I'm sorry. I won't do it again"—forgive them.[1]

JESUS

$\mathcal{B}$efore we were married, Krista and I went on a long walk on the beach, and I told her the story of a terrible thing I had done in my past. It had been before I knew her, but it was serious enough that I thought she deserved to know. If she didn't want to get married, or if she wanted to take more time, that would be okay. That would make sense. Forgiveness, after all, isn't something we get to demand from another person. It's their choice.

Forgiveness so often feels like an extraordinary, impossible thing. We marvel at these amazing stories where someone forgives the man who murdered their child, or the drunk driver who killed their husband, or the person who crippled them in an accident. I don't know what I would do in a situation like that, and hopefully most of us won't be faced with that kind of extreme situation. More often forgiveness is part of the everyday, and with people we are (or have been) close to. And it is the people closest to us who most often need our forgiveness.

Forgiveness is about restoring broken relationship. Every time I choose not to forgive someone, I'm cordoning off a piece of our relationship, small or large, and saying, "That's broken, and we're not going to fix it."

Without forgiveness, our relationships begin to suffer under the weight of the pain, anger, guilt, frustration, fear, and continued harm. Eventually—maybe soon, maybe later—our relationship collapses, possibly for good, when "one more" harm is done. And sometimes, sure, that's actually the right thing to do. Let it collapse, let it go. But let's be self-aware enough to own this: When I decide not to forgive, I'm purposely opening the door to ending this relationship.

Ultimately, forgiveness is a gift. A gift to another person, and a gift to ourselves. It's a kind of reset, a do-over, that allows us to vent away toxic and difficult emotions in our relationships. We get to say, "Let's start again but do it right this time." It allows us to express our displeasure and hurt, how we've been wronged, and then say, "The things I love about this relationship are more important than the hurt that has come from this action." It's a gift in the most literal sense. That's even where the word comes from in

English. The original Latin word, *perdonare*, means "to give wholeheartedly." When it got translated into the language that would become English, they just copied it over: *per* was translated as *for*, *donare* as *give*. Forgive.[2]

Forgiveness is a gift that says, "Yes, you messed up. But I'm not going to stop being in relationship with you because of it." There may be consequences for wounding actions or words. Whatever broke the relationship initially might change the way we interact or alter our relationship moving forward (and there are times when forgiveness does not mean a return to relationship; see the note on abuse on page 167). But when I extend forgiveness, I'm saying, "This doesn't have to be something that contributes to the end of our relationship."

Krista told me at the end of our walk that she forgave me. That she still wanted to be in relationship. That she still wanted to get married. That was a beautiful moment, and I felt deeply loved.

The journey to love always travels through forgiveness, on all sides. We are not perfect people, and neither are the people we love. Forgiveness allows the ties of relationship to grow stronger in the mending of what was broken. When we receive forgiveness, it's a reminder that although we have our issues—we are broken—we are still worthy of love. Extending forgiveness is an act of generosity and can even be tied in with patience: "I know we can do better than this. Let's try again."

REFLECTION

How has forgiveness intersected with your life? Reflect on a moment when you forgave or were forgiven, or a moment when you wanted to be forgiven or to forgive, and that didn't happen.

EXERCISE

Set an empty chair in front of you. Imagine the person you find hardest to forgive in that chair. Tell them everything: how they hurt you, the consequences of that, what you are feeling today. When you've said it all, switch chairs and role-play what they might say back to you. Don't be afraid to switch back and forth a few times. Try to imagine at least an acknowledgment of the harm done to you, if not an apology.

PART THREE

That's Not Love

Victoria read her piece aloud
in our creative-writing class
Her husband
who she had married
at sixteen
tore after her red truck
on the highway
ran her
off the road
flung open
her door
and screamed
at her
PUT ON YOUR SEAT BELT
Isn't it amazing
how much my husband
loves me
she asked
And we were
so young
And breathless
with shock
And did not know
what to say

11

LOVE IS NOT PEACE

I believe firmly that to practice love is to disrupt the status quo which is masquerading as peace.

AUSTIN CHANNING BROWN

$\mathcal{S}$ometimes love is loud.

My daughters don't always tell me about little injustices at school because, as my daughter Allie says, "I know you will go burn things down." Not literally, of course. But if someone mistreats my kids, I don't think it's loving to be polite to them about it.

We get confused sometimes and think that love means being *nice*. Sure. Sometimes. Then there are other times when people tell you, "That's not loving," but what they mean is "Don't rock the boat."

I've found it helpful to differentiate between "peace" as we think of it and the Jewish idea of "shalom." Some people, when they say "peace," mean an absence of conflict. There are a lot of ways peace (in that sense) can be achieved: the threat of violence, for instance. Imagine a plantation in the time of chattel slavery. It might have been "peaceful," but it wasn't loving or just or right.

But shalom is the idea that "all is right with the world." Everything is in its proper place. Everyone is cared for. Everyone has what they need. There is justice, and all are treated with kindness. When someone says "shalom" to you, that's what they're saying: "May God put everything in its proper place." It's a very specific kind of peace.

Sometimes we mistake the absence of conflict for peace. We say, "Oh, no one's fighting—we must be in a good place." But that might be a dishonest place. Or an unjust place. Or an unsafe place. Or a frightened place. In other words, that might be a place that has neither conflict nor love.

Let me give you an easy example. When I was a high school teacher, one of my students came to class wearing sunglasses. I asked her to take them off and saw that she had a black eye. A family member had hit her in the face. She begged me not to make a big deal about it.

Now, to avoid conflict here would have been easy. I just wouldn't tell anyone, and I could "preserve the status quo." But in this case, the status quo was causing harm to someone. Was it loving for me to keep quiet?

No.

So I called child protective services, who sent someone that same day. Then there was counseling and a lot of tears and several interviews. I don't want to go into all the details, as it's not my story to tell, but I can say this: I wouldn't call it a happy ending. Speaking up didn't magically make it all better.

But I have no question that it was the loving thing to do in that moment.

We live in a world where the status quo—for individuals, communities, ethnicities, social classes, genders, orientations, religions, nationalities—is often unjust. There are people out there who will tell you to leave it be, to stay quiet, who will say, "Don't rock the boat."

That's not love. Sometimes love challenges. Sometimes love speaks up when there's pressure to be silent. Sometimes love is loud.

REFLECTION

Are you experiencing an absence of conflict in a relationship and calling it peace? What might it look like if love stepped into that relationship?

EXERCISE

Pick an activist you respect, whether from current events or from history, and do a little research on their story. What got them started? Why were they so passionate about the change they were working to make? Do you think love had something to do with it?

12

LOVE IS NOT JEALOUS

In true love, there's no more separation or discrimination. His happiness is your happiness. Your suffering is his suffering.

THICH NHAT HANH

When I was in college, I dated a woman for several years. We were very close. Over time, our relationship became less healthy for a variety of reasons that don't really matter—and I was determined to "stick it out." We still loved each other, for one thing. It seemed like maybe, in time, we could find a way through everything.

One afternoon she sat down with me and laid it all out. The relationship wasn't healthy *for me*. She could see how I was destroying myself to try to make it work. She told me that she loved me. Really loved me, and hoped we could stay in relationship, could be friends . . . but it was time to admit that this romantic relationship was not what was best.

A jealous person would have rearranged everything to try

to keep things together in that relationship. But she loved me enough to break up with me. Not that I appreciated it or was happy about it at the time. At another time, it might have been different, or if we had some different skills or were at a different place in life. If we had been married, it would have been different. But in that moment, she was absolutely right. Yes, we both experienced some jealousy—*I wish that were me*—when we started dating other people. But what my girlfriend had said to me in that moment was, "I want what's best for you. And today, right now, us being in a romantic relationship is not what's best."

Jealousy is about what I want. Love is about what's best for you.

When we get down to it, all jealousy has the same core insecurity. It's centered on ourselves, our needs and desires. We look at others who get good things and ask, *Why them? What's so great about them? What did I do wrong? What's so terrible about me?*

When my friend gets a big promotion at work and I feel jealous, it's not because of my love for him. It's because I wish I was the one who got the promotion. He has it, and I want it. There's no room for love there because I am focused on my needs, my desires, my wants. And my jealous mind says to me, *Since he has it, you can't have it.* I don't think, *Oh, I should look for a similar job somewhere else.* I am much more likely to start comparing myself to him in unfavorable ways. *But he is late all the time, and I'm punctual.*

Jealousy is about scarcity. Love is about abundance.

When someone we love has something good come into their life, we celebrate. We work hard to center their well-being, not our own. Awards or praise, raises or promotions, new children or new opportunities. We can mourn our lack of those same things, but that's separate. We would never try to change places with them because we love them. We are so glad that they have this wonderful thing in their life.

Love is not jealous.

REFLECTION
Do you have a specific friend or family member whom you find yourself—even internally—competing with out of jealousy? Why is that? Is there a way to replace those jealous thoughts with wishes for that person's well-being?

EXERCISE
Jealousy often has an accompanying narrative in our minds: *Jim doesn't deserve that job.* As jealous thoughts come to mind, try telling the story another way: *Our boss sees something cool in Jim. What is that?* Or, *I am so thankful Jim got the job that he wanted. I hope I can get something similar in the future.* Changing the way you think about the situation can change the way you feel about it too.

13

LOVE IS NOT EASILY ANGERED

A heart full of anger has no room for love.
AS QUOTED BY JOAN LUNDEN

At the beginning of this section, I wrote about Victoria, who shared a short story with our creative-writing class about her husband tearing after her on the highway, pushing her vehicle off the road, and then screaming at her that she needed to have her seat belt on. We all sort of felt our way toward telling her, "Actually, that's a really weird response from your husband."

She asked me later, "Does that seem . . . *abusive* to you?"

And I told her, yes, your husband literally pushing your car off the road is not only abusive, it's illegal and dangerous. She took that pretty hard, but it seemed like she really wanted to know. They had been married about three years at this point.

"But he really loves me," she said. I didn't have an answer to that.

Five years later, she invited me over to her house to catch up. She had a couple kids at this point. We hadn't ever been close friends but had kept loosely in touch. I was sitting on her couch, and she was sitting in the armchair diagonal from me. She was drinking some tea, and I had some water, and we were just chatting about life. I was married now too. She had been working at a local grade school.

Victoria was so jumpy. Every time the kids made a noise, I thought she would drop her tea, and she kept looking at the front door with an expression I could only describe as fearful. I asked her, as gently as I could, "Victoria. Does your husband know that I'm visiting today?"

She assured me that he did. So I asked her, "Why are you so nervous right now?"

"Well, it's just that he might come home. Leave work without telling me. Try to surprise me."

"And . . . why would that be bad?"

"I'll be doing something wrong. He'll say I'm doing something wrong."

"This isn't normal," I told her. "Something is wrong, but it's not you."

"You don't understand," she said. "He loves me so much."

But he didn't. He did not love her. May not have ever loved her. He was an abuser, and what he enjoyed was the power and control he had over Victoria. I didn't say that to her. Instead, I quoted St. Paul, who said, "Love . . . is not easily angered."[1] *That's not love.*

He did come home. For just a handful of minutes. Long

enough to tell her, "You didn't tell me Matt was coming over" and "We can talk about this later." She and I both took that to be a threat. He yelled at the kids that they were being too loud. Then he left. He had somehow known exactly when I would be there, though. He hadn't seemed a bit surprised.

This is an extreme example because it's not just a moment of anger—it's a relationship built around abuse by a manipulative person.* And if that's where you are, please know: That's not love. You deserve better. You can get out and be safe, and there are so many resources available to help you when you're ready.

But even on a smaller scale, anger chokes love out. How can you be patient or gentle or kind or forgiving when you are always angry at the person you supposedly love?

We can be angry for a time, certainly. And some of us—like me—have a harder time dealing with anger than others. But we have to learn to control it, to tame it, to deal with it. And yes, we can direct anger in constructive ways: to protect those we love, to bring justice, to defend the defenseless.

But anger is not, and never has been, an attribute of love.

REFLECTION

Anger isn't always the primary emotion when we get mad. Sometimes it is motivated by something deeper:

---

* Abusive and manipulative people will use the beautiful impulses of loving people—forgiveness, patience, selflessness—to control the person being abused. See the note on abuse on page 167.

fear, for instance. When are you personally most likely to get angry? What sets it off?

EXERCISE

If you struggle with anger, remember: Love diffuses anger. But even when we are angry, we can practice gentleness. Reread entry 7. Make a plan for next time you are angry: How can you, even in the midst of anger, practice loving gentleness?

If a loved one struggles with anger: Every time they get angry, ask yourself, *Is this anger motivated by love?* That's it. You don't have to say anything or do anything. Just ask yourself the question.

14

LOVE IS NOT SELFISH

As selfishness and complaint pervert and cloud the mind,
so love with its joy clears and sharpens the vision.
HELEN KELLER

*W*hen Shasta was going through chemo, I'd often go to her condo and pick her up for her treatments. Once the treatments had been going for a while, she'd feel pretty sick afterward, so I'd bring her home, help her get settled, and make sure she had some ready-made food to eat if she was up for it.

She often went without a meal on those days because she was either too weak or too nauseous to eat. I had never mentioned it, but she knew that on those days, I would often skip eating, too, because I didn't want to leave her while she was getting her treatment. And, because a lot of people in the treatment room were sensitive to smell, I didn't want to bring my lunch into the hospital.

More than once, we'd get back to her place and she'd

tell me to go look in the microwave (she used her micro-wave as a cabinet because she didn't like heating things in it), and it would be full of my favorite snacks: tortilla chips, white-chocolate-chip cookies, dates, macadamia nuts. At this point, I was often doing her grocery shopping, too, which meant she had made a special trip out to get these things for me.

It was a really sweet, loving thing.

If I had been focused only on myself . . . well, for one, I wouldn't have been at that chemo treatment. I wouldn't have skipped a meal that day. The more focused we get on our own needs, the more they loom up as the only thing we can think about or reflect on. We start to notice which of our needs are unmet. We start to insist that what I need is more important than what you need, and soon we can't even make compromises. It's "my way or the highway." We get to a place where we insist that if our needs can't be put at the center, then we should break our relationship.

But if I had focused only on myself . . . I would have missed out on Shasta's kindness. Being self-focused doesn't just prevent us from giving love—it prevents us from receiving it too.

When we focus on others' needs, we leave space for people we love to think about *our* needs. By thinking about the needs of others and leaving some of my own unmet, I opened up a place for Shasta to show her care for me.

Something I struggle with is letting other people know what my needs are, but that's part of this too. I am learning that when my friends or family ask, "Do you need anything?" or "How are you doing?" I have to be vulnerable enough to answer those questions honestly. Honesty is caring for the needs of others because it invites them to participate in our needs, just as we participate in theirs. It's a vulnerability we invite our loved ones into, and they show their love by helping us receive what we are lacking.

As we link ourselves in relationships to others by seeking to care for them and allowing them to meet our needs, we also naturally build an ever-widening circle of caring community. We move from being self-focused to focusing on others, and as others do the same, we build a group of people all taking care of one another's needs. We connect loved ones who have complementary needs or abilities. A friend needs something fixed in their house, and we realize that another friend, who loves to serve others through that kind of work, could help meet that need. A friend is trying to get a book published, and we think, *Oh, I should introduce them to Matt.* As we let our needs be known, the community begins to problem solve: How do we find a solution for not just "Matt's need" but *this* need in our group? We draw overlapping circles of more and more people connected, noticing, and caring for one another's needs.

At one point during Shasta's treatment, she didn't have the financial resources to keep going, and she was pretty stressed about it. Her friends got together and held a fundraiser, and many, many people—some who didn't even know her—donated.

All those people, family and friends and strangers, decided that instead of using that money on themselves, they would use it for her. They saw her need, and they wanted to meet it, and the impact multiplied beyond even her immediate community. That's a fascinating thing about love—it keeps creating more space for itself. It spreads and grows.

Love is not selfish. Love gives, and grows, and receives . . . and gives again.

REFLECTION
If you turned your focus completely on the people around you, do you believe—really believe—that your personal needs would still be met? Why or why not?

EXERCISE
Think back on the last twenty-four hours. Which of your actions, words, and decisions were driven by self-interest, self-focus, or selfishness? How might your day have looked different if you had made different choices in those moments?

15

LOVE DOESN'T SHAME OR DISHONOR

The supreme happiness of life is the conviction that we are loved;
loved for ourselves—say rather, loved in spite of ourselves.
VICTOR HUGO

*O*nce, when we traveled to Costa Rica with friends, Krista's backpack was stolen. She was with her friend at a local café, they closed their eyes to pray together for a moment, and the thief snuck in and snatched the backpack. Krista came and found me—I was with her friend's husband—and told me what happened, and I asked her, "Are you okay?"

She was fine, just upset about her bag. We went back and looked around in the neighborhood, thinking maybe someone would have abandoned the bag after taking everything inside, but they hadn't. It was gone.

The friend's husband pulled me aside later. "Shouldn't you have yelled at Krista a little? Or made her feel bad for what happened?"

Well, no. She already felt bad, for one. I asked him more about what was behind his question, and he told me that in his family growing up, if you messed up, everyone would make sure you knew you had messed up. It would be pointed out, explained, dissected, publicly displayed, and discussed at length. By the end, he said, you would feel so stupid that you knew you could never mess up like that again.

I told him that I understood why he had the perspective he did, and we laid out the situation again. Could Krista control that someone else had taken her backpack? Had she done anything wrong? Was she more important than anything that was lost in that moment?

Of course, he said, I was right. He told me he needed to think about this because his default in these moments had been built by his family growing up, and he wanted to change it.

We could have gone a step further. What if it *had* been Krista's fault in some way? What if she had not been paying attention and had gotten in a car accident? What if she had purposely broken something or thrown away something important?

Those things might have been upsetting, but because I love her, I hope that I wouldn't publicly shame or dishonor her. When we love someone, we want to platform their best skills, abilities, and characteristics when we talk about them. Not that we're unaware of their worst qualities or never speak of them. In fact, we are more aware of those things in our close relationships than we are in casual relationships. It's just that we don't shame people for not being perfect, or for being in a growth process (or even stuck with some character issues). On the contrary, to love them fully requires not only that we know and love what is broken and worst about our loved ones, but that we love them despite those things.

More than once, I've gathered the courage to go to a loved one to admit to them one of my own issues, only to be met with a laugh and a hug and some comment to the effect of, "You think I didn't already know this about you?"

There is power in knowing *my sibling/spouse/parent/friend knows the worst things about me and still loves me anyway.* No matter how broken or terrible we think we are, we can still be loved and still receive that love.

REFLECTION
Imagine someone you love came to you and told you their backpack had been stolen. Would you be more likely to respond with shame or judgment, or with concern?

EXERCISE
Be watching for examples of how the people around you—in your family, community, workplace—treat others who experience failures or have character weaknesses. Is public shaming or dishonoring of people the norm? Or is something else? Reflect on how the environments that influence you may or may not be affecting your own journey toward love.

PART FOUR

The Power of Love

Virgil says,
"Love conquers all,"
or more exactly
omnia vincit amor,
to which the internet
and the burnt-out skeptic
and yes sometimes I
say "Ten Myths
We Must Destroy
about Love."
And we fight and bluster
and build our barricades
and set our bayonets
and load our bullets.
Let's see love conquer us.
Virgil watches,
an amused expression
on his face and says,
"Love conquers all,
so we must surrender to love."
Our bullets never touch love,
they just whistle straight through.
Our bayonets can't keep it away.
And over our barricades
a small white flag is already flying.

16

THE POWER OF TRUTH

love is the voice under all silences,
the hope which has no opposite in fear;
the strength so strong mere force is feebleness:
the truth more first than sun more last than star

E. E. CUMMINGS

$\mathcal{M}$y psych teacher in college loved to give us these "moral conundrums" so she could study us as we tried to figure out what to do. We did the "lifeboat" game where you look at a list of people on a ship and choose which ones to save. We did exercises where you had to decide whether to accept one person's sacrifice so two people could live. We explored the "trolley problem"—the premise is that a runaway trolley is on a switch track: Do you kill everyone on the trolley, or switch tracks so only a child is killed? Things like that.

She also liked to quiz us on lying. Are there times when lying is the moral choice? For instance, was it okay to lie to the Nazis during World War II if you were hiding Jewish people in your house? All of which set us off into a philosophical wonderland of what lying is, when and if it's acceptable, and so on.

But our question here is simpler: Is it loving to tell lies?

The classic setup in our psych class had to do with Grandma. You take your grandma to the store. She's trying on dresses. There's one she really loves. You don't think it looks good on her, but you don't want to hurt her feelings. Do you tell her you like it?

It's an interesting question because on the one hand, we have the moral issue (i.e., lying) and on the other, *Should I hurt Grandma's feelings over this little thing?* But love moves us toward truth—not as an exercise in morality or because of hurt feelings, but because love knows that compassionate honesty creates more space for relationship.

Love takes a bigger view. I love Grandma, and I'm going to be in relationship with her until one of us dies. I'm not going anywhere. What if I say, "Sure, you look great," and she buys the dress—but it's not actually flattering at all? Will someone else say something to hurt her feelings when she wears it later? Have I caused her more pain then? Would it be preferable to say, "Grandma, I think we can find something better"?

This gets complicated because some people use truth as a weapon. They say something hurtful and defend themselves with "I'm just being honest." That's not what we're talking about here. People sometimes say true things in a way that is not loving.

But love and truth are all wrapped together. How can I love someone I fundamentally distrust? How can I trust someone who isn't loving? My closest friends—people whom I've chosen to be in loving relationship with—are the most brutally honest with me about myself. Sometimes that's about negative things ("Matt, you're being a jerk right now"), and sometimes it's helping me see myself more honestly ("Matt, you're not giving yourself enough credit"). Krista doesn't pretend to like something I've done just because I did it. She's quick to point out how things could be better. JR. often tells me I need to take better care of myself or points out my own inconsistencies. My kids *love* to tease me about my quirks and inconsistencies. Shasta always told me things straight-out.

And love is a true thing. It exists, and it shines light into the furthest corners of our hearts. Love doesn't shrink away when it discovers something strange or malformed in our lives. It heals, it patiently waits for change, and it stays whether change happens or not. We hide ourselves from love because we think love isn't strong enough to know our true selves. But love is stronger than that. Love is more powerful than any lie.

An ancient Hebrew proverb says, "The wounds of a friend are faithful."[1] Loving truth makes us better, heals us, moves us toward greater love. The truth hurts sometimes, but when delivered by someone who loves us, it's hurt that leads to something better.

REFLECTION

Do you want the people closest to you to be honest with you? Do you think they want the same thing from you? What is an example of a time someone close to you was honest, and you felt loved? How about a time someone lied, and you felt hurt or betrayed?

EXERCISE

Take one day and don't say anything untrue. No exaggerations, no "white lies," no false comments to save someone's feelings. You don't have to volunteer information you think will hurt someone, but don't lie, either. If you must deliver a painful truth, do it with sensitivity, kindness, and love.

17

THE POWER OF HOPE

Love recognizes no barriers. It jumps hurdles, leaps fences,
penetrates walls to arrive at its destination full of hope.
MAYA ANGELOU

*W*hen we were newly dating, Krista went away for a few days to a teachers' conference. We didn't have a way to stay in touch during this time. I was feeling insecure in our relationship—mostly because of this nagging feeling that my previous romantic relationships had failed "once she got to know the real me." That wasn't true, by the way, but I felt like it was. And I was convinced that when Krista got back from the conference, she was going to break up with me.

What I didn't recognize at the time was that this revealed an issue with me, not an issue with Krista. What it boiled down to, honestly, was the belief that she didn't actually love me. Love would stick with me even if it discovered something in me that needed some work. But I didn't have faith in her love.

Now, if I compared this with how I felt about my parents, you could see how ridiculous it would be. As I've mentioned before, my parents have been these extraordinarily loving people in my life. My sisters, too! If my parents and sisters went away for three days and I had no way to contact them, it wouldn't even cross my mind that they would return from the trip and say, "We're done with you." Of course not!

Hope is a type of faith. Faith is the belief that something works the way it's intended to, or that something or someone is trustworthy. I have faith that a chair will hold me when I sit down in it. Faith tells me that when Krista says, "I love you," she knows what that means and says it with good intentions.

Hope is faith extended into the future. Hope takes what is presently believed in faith (*This person loves me.*) and says, *That will still be true in twenty years.* Or tomorrow or next week or even sixty years from now.

Hope can be about even better things coming too. If we believe in the transformational ability of love, we can look at our loved ones and see them not just for who they are today, but for who they are becoming. I look at my daughters and see not just the wonderful people they are right now, but the incredible potential they have to be astonishing people in the future. Hope doesn't just think that things will "still be good" one day but that they're going to get even better.

Hope, in that sense, is a unique and important aspect of

love. It connects our present and our future. The inability to predict the future creates a lot of stress, fear, and uncertainty in our lives. Hope alleviates that. Hope comforts us. Hope reminds us how strong love is, and that it will overcome barriers that arise in our future.

Here's an example: One place I consistently see hopelessness is in politics. There's a lot of fear and uncertainty based on who ends up in power (and rightfully so). In the United States, that feeling of hopefulness or hopelessness tends to go in four-year cycles. During our recent presidential election, a friend put together a "support group" for some like-minded friends to text each other through the day as we waited for the election results. Though I only knew a few of the people on the chain to start, as we waited for the results to come in and shared our fears, concerns, and desires, I started to feel some hope. Even if my candidate didn't win, here were some people like me . . . some people who cared about things that I care about, people who— whatever happens with the election—are going to be there in the months and years to come. There's precious little hope in politics, and precious little love . . . but among our fellow humans, we find both hope and love because we say to ourselves, *Whatever comes, I know these people who love me will still be there.*

Hope is an act of future certainty based in what we know to be true today. And, sometimes, what has been proven to be true in the past. When we look back on the effect of love in our relationships in the past, we become more certain of love's continued effect into the future. Love connects the past to the present, the present to the future.

St. Paul said, "Love . . . always hopes."[1] Love created hopefulness in our past. Love generates hope in our present. Love extends hope into our future.

REFLECTION

Given what we've learned about hope, what would a hopeful person look and sound like?

EXERCISE

Take some time privately to make a list of your five deepest fears in relationships. These can be specific to an individual relationship (like mine with Krista when we were dating) or a broad generality. How could the power of hope transform those fears?

18

THE POWER
OF COURAGE

Being deeply loved by someone gives you strength,
while loving someone deeply gives you courage.

LAO-TZU

I'm afraid of sharks. I don't like going in the ocean above my waist. When I was a kid and wanted a shot of adrenaline, I would go to our swimming pool at night, turn off all the lights, jump in the deep end, and then thrash my way out. I just knew there would be a shark—a great white—in our pool somehow.

This phobia of sharks has been around for a long time, and it's going to stick with me. But I guarantee you, if someone tossed one of my daughters into a vat of sharks, I would, without thinking, jump in after her to try to pull her out. Love gives me courage.

When we build loving relationships, there are lots of opportunities for fear. Fear of rejection, fear of loss, fear of change. But the strength of love overcomes fear. Washes it away. As St. John wrote, "Perfect love casts out fear."[1] Or maybe we could say it another way: Love makes us courageous.

Some of the greatest events in history have grown out of a love that destroys fear, that pushes back against the terror of standing up for what is right. The civil rights movement, for example, grew out of a desire to make sure that people were treated with the love and respect they deserved as fellow human beings. The courage of love can be like that—stepping out and speaking up for those who are being mistreated in some way, whether in a personal or a community context.

Love also calms our fears about ourselves. When we know that someone deeply and truly loves us, we don't spend a lot of emotional energy being scared that it will go away somehow. That confidence, that strength, gives us a core courage to do other things. It makes us more sure of ourselves, more capable.

Love removes our fear of punishment for being who we are, letting us move toward the courage of honesty, of sharing the reality of who we are, who we have been, and who we are becoming. We don't need to hide ourselves from those who love us.

In this sense, our fears can be instructive about where we do not feel loved or are uncertain that we are loved. For instance, I hate asking for help. I don't like to ask for money, help doing yardwork, or even simple things—like telling my friends something I would like to do or taking the opportunity to rest when I am overtired. I don't even like to write this, but that's all rooted in fear. Fear that I need to be useful to be loved. Fear that people don't want to help me. Fear that people don't see me as worth their time, energy, money, and so on.

My uncertainty in love is partially that I am failing to

love myself. I see my own worth differently than those who love me do. Which means that I often fail to take courageous actions for me that I would easily and gladly take for others. I think a lot of us experience this.

Now, in my closest relationships—my parents and sisters, Krista and the kids, my in-laws, my best friends—this is less true. Because my certainty of their love overpowers my fears. But the fear I feel points out to me a place in my life where love has not fully penetrated.

Because where there is love, there is courage.

REFLECTION

Where do you most often see courageous action in your life? Where do you most often experience fear in relationships?

EXERCISE

Once you've identified a place of fear in your life, choose one courageous thing you've always wanted to do that is in opposition to that fear. It can be something you've wanted to tell someone, a life change you've wanted to make, a secret you want to be rid of, a gift you've wanted to give, a huge thing or a small thing. Now take a step toward that thing. You don't have to do the thing itself. But do something that moves you toward doing that thing, and see how you feel.

19

THE POWER OF
ENDURANCE

If you have a love for something, you persevere.
ADEBAYO AKINFENWA

When you're going to the hospital multiple times a week over the course of years, you see some really sad things. For a lot of Shasta's appointments, I would go in with her, but there were always some where visitors weren't allowed. Radiation was one of those.

During one such radiation appointment, I was sitting outside the radiation office and struck up a conversation with an older woman who was there. She was playing with a tablet, and she turned and looked at me and said, "You don't happen to read Chinese, do you?"

Which was such a random question. But, strangely enough, I do read a little bit of Chinese, so I told her that I did. She showed me her tablet. "Well, somehow I turned the language on this thing to Chinese."

Now, she was in luck, because one of a short list of words

I know in Chinese is "English." I was able to find the menu, get to languages, and set it to English. She was thrilled. It had been stuck on Chinese for three days.

"Are you waiting for someone?" I asked.

"Oh, just my ride home." It turned out that she was waiting for a cab. She had just finished radiation treatment and was headed back to an assisted-living place. She told me that all her loved ones had passed away or lived too far off to come help her with doctor's appointments or tablets changing languages.

Which was really different from Shasta's life. She might have gone to two appointments by herself in the entire four years of her treatment. A decent-sized list of people took turns taking care of her, staying with her, helping with things she needed. She had several close friends who joined her for appointments, or dropped in to take her on walks, or just sent her funny David Hasselhoff videos (she loved the Hoff). And some of those people were with her not just those four years but for her entire life—her parents and brother in particular.

Still, there were people who disappeared. Being close to someone who is sick for the long term is painful. Some people had to tap out. They stopped calling, or inviting her out to things, or checking in on her. Shasta didn't like it, but she understood. With some people, it hurt more than others. She often said it had been really clarifying about who her true friends were. Because love doesn't give up. Love doesn't fail. Love sticks it out, even when things are at their worst.

Shasta asked me once, "Will you walk me to the door?" She meant the door out of this life and into the next. When she asked me that, I was surprised, because I thought that had already been clear.

When there are questions like that, love says yes.

Love says yes because love endures all things. That's the other side of "never failing." It's going on, going forward, not giving up. That endurance is underneath all the other things that are powerful about love. We can speak truth because truth is invested in the long term, in sticking with someone even when truth is hard. Hope requires perseverance, a looking ahead and trusting in the future. Courage requires the certainty, constancy, consistency of love to chase away fear.

Love is a power unlike any other in the world. It never fails. Never gives up. Never ceases. Love always has been, always is, and always will be.

REFLECTION

What is the longest loving relationship you know? This could be someone you're in a loving relationship with, or someone else you know and have observed. What do you think helps them "stick it out" in love?

EXERCISE

Reach out to someone (a stranger or someone you know) who has a long-standing loving relationship (with a parent, child, spouse, friend . . . any kind of relationship) that you find compelling. Ask if you can interview them about long-term relationships.

20

LOVE AND DEATH

Love is as strong as death.[1]
KING SOLOMON

$\mathcal{W}$hat is the opposite of love?

It's not hatred. Hatred is weak. Love easily defeats it.

Some people say indifference is the opposite of love, but indifference also is weak. It's an absence.

I believe love's opposite is death.

Death is powerful. Every person on earth will one day experience it. Death is inevitable and all-encompassing. Death is an either/or. You don't become "partially dead." You are alive or you are not alive.

But love is powerful too. Every person on earth experiences it. Love is inevitable and all-encompassing. Love is an either/or. You can't be "partially loved." Someone either loves you or does not. You are loving or not loving.

I know you may not have experienced this "inevitable" love. You may say to yourself, "If it's inevitable, why don't I have it now?" Listen, friend, you're not dead now, either. Do you believe that death will come for you in time? It certainly will, whether you believe it or not, and whether you fight it or not. Love is like that. Believe it or not, fight it or not, love is coming for you. Love is as strong as death.

Love can't *stop* death, obviously. Anyone who has lost a loved one will tell you that. But *death doesn't stop love*, either. Anyone who has lost a loved one will tell you that, too.

I can make a list of loved ones I have lost. Shasta, of course. My grandparents. Good friends who are gone. And I can make a list, too, of the loved ones I will someday lose. But that list is more difficult. I might die before them.

One of the last times Shasta and I spent together was after she had lost most of her strength to walk. Her loving parents had come to stay with her and were caring for her. She asked if I could come help her with a work thing—she needed to return something to the store. So I picked her up and we went and did that, and afterward we went to a little park in Portland. I set out her wheelchair and rolled her next to a bench, where I sat and we looked down on a series of small ponds covered in lilies.

And she told me that—after four years of fighting—she would be stopping her treatment. It wasn't working any-more, anyway, and it was making her sick. She had tried everything. Now it was time to finish the journey. We both started to cry, and I took her hand, and we just watched the lilies and the people walking around the park for a few minutes.

When I was driving her home, we talked about our families and about saying goodbye. I told her I would miss her, and she said she knew that was true. And she asked me if I had any regrets. Regrets about spending the last four years on this journey with her now that we knew how it was going to end.

And you know what? I didn't. Not a single regret. Because she was my friend, and I love her. Love is as strong as death. Stronger, I think. Death has done its worst, but love is still here.

Maybe you've already experienced that.

If you haven't, you most certainly will.

Sometimes we think death is stronger than love. We choose to step back from a relationship because of fear that we will lose that person. Or we suspect that when death comes, love will go. We're worried about the pain that will come if we lose someone we love.

But I can tell you . . . death is hard, but living without love is harder.

Don't let death keep you from loving. Love is more powerful than that.

REFLECTION

Are you skeptical that love will come for everyone? Do you believe it's as inevitable, as strong as death? If not, why not? If so, what are some of the ramifications of that?

EXERCISE

We can't predict when death will come. We don't all get the luxury of saying goodbye. Write a letter to someone you love and hide it somewhere where they won't find it, or seal it and give it to a mutual friend. Leave a shout of love hidden away in case death meets you when you don't expect it.

PART FIVE

Barriers to Love

He got off the plane
in the country of Love.
His papers all in order.
Passport, visa, customs declaration.
Looked around for border patrol,
couldn't find them, kept asking.
No one seemed to know
what he was talking about.
"Just walk through the door,"
they said and he, helpless,
held up his passport.
"I can't without proper permission."
Five hours later, a woman
with a makeshift uniform
found him and glanced
through his documents.
"Everything is in order here,"
she said and handed them back.
"I can go in now?" he asked,
and she replied, "Our job
isn't to keep you out;
it's to help you realize
that you're already here."

21

RUDENESS

*Life's most persistent and urgent question is,
"What are you doing for others?"*
MARTIN LUTHER KING JR.

I took a class in high school that taught us all about cultural politeness rules: how to set a table, which spoon to use when, how to address a letter to someone respectfully. It always seemed like ridiculous, antiquated nitpicking to me. But years later, I was reading an advice column—for some reason those always entertain me—and the woman writing the column said something to the effect that good manners are never about following the little rules about the silverware but always about remembering the Golden Rule: Treat others how you would want to be treated. She went on to say that, in fact, it could be rude to insist on "the rules of good manners" if it caused harm or embarrassment to someone.

This is why, she said, one never publicly draws attention to a faux pas. That in and of itself would be poor manners.

So it may seem strange to say that rudeness is something in our lives that reveals a place where we are fighting against love. It's a barrier to love, a way we keep love out of our lives. When we are consistently rude, it shows that we are not thinking of others. We are thinking of ourselves.

I'm not suggesting, of course, that if you use your salad fork to eat your steak, you're lacking in love. But think of it like this: When I go out to a restaurant with others, there's a spectrum in how people treat their servers. Some people act as though servers are some sort of robotic extension of the restaurant itself: There's a brief transaction, and then one's food arrives. Some treat their servers unkindly, or with rudeness—which is to say, in a way that is not loving. In fact, I've seen people behave toward their servers in a way that seems to communicate a core disrespect: not treating them as human beings.

And then there are people like my friend Glen. When we go to a restaurant and the server comes up and says, "Hello, my name is Tracy," he says, "Hello, Tracy, my name is Glen." The first time I went to a restaurant with him, I was so taken aback by this, and it made me realize how normal it should be. If Tracy shares her name with us, why would we not share our names with her? Glen is always unfailingly kind to his servers, and he always tips well too.

Rudeness is not unloving in and of itself. There are times to cut through all the pleasantries. If someone is having a heart attack, you don't need to spend a lot of time saying hello to the emergency crew as they show up. But consistent rudeness can be an indication of something deeper: a profound difficulty in seeing and responding to the needs of other people.

You can see that the quote at the beginning of this reflection is from Martin Luther King Jr., a man who was well known for seeking far more than politeness in his work. When school integrations were happening and supposedly loving middle-class white folks were screaming at little African American girls as they were ushered into school by protective policemen, that was something more than rudeness. When someone sprayed acid in young Melba Pattillo's eyes, when Elizabeth Eckford was shoved down a flight of stairs, that wasn't just rudeness.

But honestly, it was rude, too, wasn't it? It was worse than rudeness, yes, but no one would say that was polite behavior, would they?

If the people who did those things had been paying attention to even this little question—*Is what I'm about to do polite?*—then perhaps they would have thought twice.

This is not in any way to minimize the horrors of these sorts of acts of violence but to say that when we are rude, this is the path we are on. It is not a path of love. It is not a path of care for others.

And when we are moving toward politeness—*How would others want to be treated?*—we are, by definition, also moving toward the fight for justice in the world around us.

REFLECTION

Can you think of a time when you were rude? How about a time someone else was rude to you? Be watching for the next time you are tempted to be rude. Does the instinct come from a loving heart or not?

EXERCISE

The next time you interact with someone in a service industry—on the phone, in person, on the internet—ask yourself how you would want to be treated. Try to treat them that way and see how it feels.

22

A LACK OF VULNERABILITY

Embracing our vulnerabilities is risky but not nearly as dangerous as giving up on love and belonging and joy— the experiences that make us the most vulnerable.

BRENÉ BROWN

I love children, but the first time I held one of my own— little Zoey—was a moment of complete transformation. The kid crawled into my heart, set up a perimeter, and built her own space there. Not because she was some amazing person (though she is). Not because she had enormous strength (she couldn't actually crawl). Not because there was something I wanted or needed from her (she had literally nothing).

She was vulnerable in every sense of the word. All babies are. No ability to protect herself. Weak and in need. She wasn't even able to communicate clearly what her needs were—she cried just to make us aware, and we tried everything we could think of to discover what exactly might be the problem.

Most of us hate vulnerability, but avoiding it absolutely

creates a roadblock on the journey to love. Allowing someone to love us requires that we let them know who we are: our history, our pains, our weaknesses and fears—not just our good qualities or our strengths.

What makes vulnerability so hard is that, by definition, sharing where we are vulnerable gives other people power over us. We give them the ability to hurt us. That's why arguments with people we love are the hardest sort—our loved ones are tempted to use our vulnerabilities against us. Make no mistake: Weaponizing another's vulnerabilities is an enormous betrayal to the implicit promise of love, which is *It is safe to make yourself vulnerable to me*. This is why divorces are often so brutal and have long-term emotional, psychological, and spiritual effects. Someone who knows our vulnerabilities is exploiting them in an effort to get something from us or, sometimes, just to hurt us.

If there's not someone in your life who could hurt you badly because they know you better than others do, then chances are you are struggling to be vulnerable in your closest relationships. Think of your heart as a walled city. The places where you are vulnerable are the gates. If you never open those doors, your loved ones can't enter and deliver the things that they have for you. Of course, if you never open those gates, you can't be hurt, either.

And let's not confuse vulnerability with transparency. Vulnerability is letting someone in past your defenses. Transparency is putting a tiny window in the wall. Transparency is being honest about yourself but being careful only to share things that can't be used to hurt you. Some old story when you got embarrassed as a kid, for instance, would be transparency but not vulnerability. Sharing your needs can be vulnerability, especially needs that you are unable to fill for yourself. But if you share a need from your past that has since been taken care of, you're being transparent, not vulnerable.

But this is why vulnerability is worth it: Becoming vulnerable can also make it easier for others to love us. Many people feel an instinct to protect and care for those who are vulnerable. I am not suggesting that you create drama or manufacture vulnerabilities (some people do that) but rather that allowing yourself to be cared for creates closeness in relationship. When we share our deepest vulnerabilities, it makes other people feel safe around us. We would not be giving them the ability to hurt us unless we had no plans to hurt them.

Vulnerability is all about lowering our defenses. It's a necessary part of love because when we are trying to protect ourselves from being hurt, most often that means we are protecting ourselves from love as well.

I'm the kind of person who has a lot of friends . . . lots and lots of people I'm friendly with. I'll pick up the phone when they call, and I'll hear about their problems and help them with their needs. I'm also the kind of person who uses that as a smoke screen so that I don't have to enter true, vulnerable friendship. I'll help you with your needs and not tell you anything about mine. It's common for me to know deep, difficult things others are dealing with and not share even minor issues of my own. In fact, those who've become my closest friends are often people who've called me on how I give the appearance of vulnerability without ever opening the gates. They've invited me to let them in. I'm working on it. I'm trying.

We often fear vulnerability because we think of it as giving others the power to harm us. But look at it this way: When we embrace vulnerability, we give others the power and permission to love us too.

REFLECTION

In your life, do you lean more toward vulnerability or self-protection? How does this affect your relationships? Are you satisfied with your current situation?

EXERCISE

This is going to sound strange, and it's going to feel uncomfortable—because this is an exercise in vulnerability. You'll need another human being to pull this one off. Ask someone to sit with you for four minutes and to keep eye contact the entire time. Set an alarm for four minutes and just look at each other. Don't talk. Don't "stare"—it's okay to blink. Just watch each other, eye to eye, for four minutes. When that alarm goes off, take a moment to laugh and look at something else and shake it off. Then talk about it: What was the experience like? What were you thinking? What did you feel?

23

PRIDE

Love . . . settles for less than perfection and makes
allowances for human weaknesses.
ANN LANDERS

When I say "pride," I don't mean the satisfaction that comes from a job well done or the feeling of accomplishment at the end of a long-term pursuit. I'm not talking about healthy self-respect or the idea of being a person of worth, both things that can contribute to our capacity to love and be loved. No—what I want to talk about here is the kind of pride that means having an excessively high opinion of oneself.

Pride is a barrier to love in our lives because pride refuses to admit weakness. How can I be weak if I am the best? How can I be vulnerable when I am too powerful to be hurt? When we are without weakness, we also lack a place for someone to enter into our lives. We cannot extend knowledge of ourselves, and we can't invite people to know us, because they will inevitably discover the vast space between who we pretend to be and who we actually are. Pride prevents us from vulnerability, and lack of vulnerability prevents us from being known. And because we are not known, we are skeptical even of those who truly do love us. *If they knew the "real me," they would be horrified and would not love me.* Or so we think.

Pride moves us to focus on ourselves. Any time spent looking at the people around us is only for the sake of comparison and to remind ourselves, *Oh, I am better than that person.* Because we look at other people around us only to critique and belittle them, we're unable to have meaningful, loving relationships with them. Every interaction becomes, in time, about us.

Pride is a failure to see. Because we can't admit the truth about ourselves, we also cannot admit the truth about people around us. Every step toward truth causes our carefully constructed self-image to shudder at the base, and even a small revelation of who we really are introduces pain, worry, fear, anger. We lash out at the people or circumstances that throw light on our true self. Love is grounded in truth, so the defenses we build keep out not just truth but love as well. We cannot produce love in the truest sense because we can't clearly see the needs and desires of the people around us, whom we see as worth far less than we are.

Pride also prevents us from being honest about our needs. Why would we need something? We are self-sufficient, powerful. People who need things are weak and lesser.

Because we cannot share our needs, those who love us are not able to meet us in those areas of pain and lack. In fact, people who seem to love us often are people who give us praise because "we are so great" but know nothing about us—not really. And those who truly love us see fewer and fewer places to interact in our lives, so they slowly move away emotionally, maybe not even knowing why.

This particular barrier to love can be immensely confusing, especially to those who seem to have reason for pride—the very accomplished, or famous, or wealthy. There is reason to have great compassion for people in those situations. We need to encourage them to embrace that they are still human, still people with deep needs, and that love—not just fans or people who want their money or attention—is still available to them.

Pride is a barrier to love. It fills up every inch of our lives. It doesn't leave space for anything or anyone but us. It protects us from hurt, yes, but it makes us lonely and often angry and self-focused people. Pride is often a disguise for fear. We are worth more than we think we are . . . and we are more fragile, broken, and weak than we like to admit. When we lay down our pride—even for a moment—it creates a space for love to fill.

REFLECTION

Do you deal with pride in your life? If so, is it just in one area, or is it more widespread? How do you feel when someone pushes against your image of yourself?

EXERCISE

"How can I help?" For this exercise, you need to ask other people this question. Not because you're the best, but because when we are dealing with issues of pride, it's helpful to push our focus toward others. There will be people you don't know how to help, *and that's okay*. Becoming aware of our limitations is also part of dismantling pride—and making more room for love—in our lives.

24

GRIEF

Where you used to be, there is a hole in the world,
which I find myself constantly walking around
in the daytime, and falling in at night.
EDNA ST. VINCENT MILLAY

Grief is the place where death and love intersect.

It's cinder blocks on your chest when you wake. It's having your feet in cement when someone invites you to come out of the house. It's carrying a pack of bricks throughout the day . . . to the grocery store, to work, to pick up the kids at school. It's the exhausting, invisible gravity of loss.

When Shasta died, it was like someone sawed a leg off the chair of my life. Nothing could sit right after that. In the space of a day, I went from having this person who loved me unconditionally, who knew my ins and outs, who gave me loving advice, who had been a part of my life and my family's life for decades—and she was gone. She was photographs and old text messages and memories.

My friend Alan reached out after she died—his best friend had died several years before—and said, "It will get better, but grief is on a clock." There are things you can do to make it go more smoothly, but not much you can do to make it go *faster*.

JR. and Krista kept pushing me to take care of myself. Did I eat today? Did I exercise? Was I sleeping? What was I doing to take care of myself? And every once in a while, when I pushed back on their insistence, JR. would ask, "What would Shasta want you to do?"

Which, of course, she would say those same things. I had jokingly called her "Nurse Shasta" because she was always encouraging me to be healthier. She would want me to take care of myself because she loved me.

Grief can prevent us from accepting love because the new love that comes isn't the same as the old love. I found myself asking how I could replace a friend who had been so tied into my life and family, and the answer was that I couldn't. There may be other friendships—incredible friendships—to come, but they will not be that. Not exactly.

Grief can prevent us from being loving. There is a natural self-defense mechanism that activates when we experience pain. The pain of grief is unrelenting and—while it may grow less frequent—never completely goes away. It takes so much attention, so much time.

And why does grief take time?

Because when we are carrying grief, it's not an option to set it aside. We must grow stronger and learn to carry it. While death may have taken someone we loved, grief is evidence that our love was not defeated. Grief increases our capacity to love, if we can find the strength to see it that way.

There is a Japanese art form called *kintsugi*. The way it works is this: the artist takes a broken piece of pottery—a cup or a plate, a bowl or a vase—and repairs the cracks with lacquer and precious metals. Not only do we embrace the broken places; we illuminate them. We celebrate the brokenness, and we see it as a part of the beautiful history of who we are, how we have been made in this life. Grief passes over broken hearts and leaves behind a golden seam. Love encourages us to put those broken hearts on display. And, friend, I know this is hard to believe . . . but it's actually beautiful to see.

REFLECTION
Grief comes to us all in time, which is just another way of saying that both love and death come to us in time. When have you experienced grief? Friend, that's an indication of love in your life. When do you anticipate or fear grief in your future? Friend, dive in deep to that loving relationship now, that the eventual cost of grief may be counterbalanced by the depth and beauty of love today.

EXERCISE

Do you have a friend in grief today? Know that they are desperate for even the smallest acts of love, even if they can't say it. Don't ask them what they need. Volunteer something. A prayer, a book, a meal, a kindhearted card.

Are you in grief today? Do you feel like you've been caught in a wave and dragged away from shore? Then raise your hand, and let someone on the beach know you need help. Invite them into your grief, and let them support you on the journey back to solid ground.

25

PERMISSION

Love saves us only if we want to be saved.
BELL HOOKS

$\mathcal{M}$y friend Lisa was teaching me how to drive a stick shift. We were in our twenties, and I had just told her that I was going to become a Christian missionary . . . not for a year or a summer, but as a full-time job. Lisa told me to stop the car (which was easy—I had killed the engine about a hundred times), looked me in the eye, and said, "That's a bad job for you." I asked her why and she said, "You're a loving person, that's why."

As we went deeper into the conversation, she explained to me that missionaries had one job: telling people that they were wrong about questions of faith and spirituality, and explaining to them that they should agree, instead, with the missionary.

Which, here's the thing . . . she's not completely wrong. That has been true for plenty of missionaries. Missionaries have used force, violence, bribery, bait and switch, and a hundred other immoral or questionable tactics to "convert" people to agreement.

Of course, that's doing it wrong and utterly missing the point. Because the core message of a missionary—what a Christian would call the "gospel" or Good News—starts with this idea that God loves human beings. To try to force someone to accept love from God . . . well, we have words for people who try to force love on others. We all feel gross about someone trying to "bribe" us into accepting their love. And we know that the ultimate coercion—violent love—is not love.

Love that relies on violence, force, bribery, bait and switch (etc.) is something counterfeit, something disgusting. Love has to be accepted. We have to consent to love.

Now, can people love us without our permission or even our knowledge? Sure. That happens. But to enter into loving *relationship*, to have our lives transformed by love . . . that requires our permission, our consent, and our active participation.

Have you ever lost someone you loved and found it impossible to engage with people afterward? Have you been hurt or abused and now find that you cannot trust again? Have you put everything you had into a relationship and been betrayed, and now you're skeptical of investing in anyone?

There are many potential barriers to love. Sometimes the barrier is simply that we don't have the strength to say yes.

So, what does it look like to say yes to love?

What does it look like to say no to love?

Has someone offered you friendship? An invitation to a meal or a coffee? What did you say? Have you ever been the first one to reach out to someone else?

Have you ever had a close friend get married and you realized, *That person's spouse will now have to be my friend too*, and decided—before you even met them—to let them into your inner circle?

Maybe you've been blessed with one of those moments where you immediately connected with someone and were tempted to say, "I think we should be friends." Maybe they said it to you.

Have you ever had someone tell you that they love you and you just froze for a moment, not sure if you should say it back?

Each of these are choices, decisions, offerings to enter into someone else's life. We can offer, or not. They can accept, or not. Anything that is demanded cannot be love. But the other side of acceptance is the potential for love.

REFLECTION

When have you said yes to love? When have you said no? What was the result?

EXERCISE

Say yes to an invitation toward love today. And give someone else an opportunity to respond to an invitation to loving relationship from you.

PART SIX

Divine Love

Someone said, "God is love"
and I wonder does
that mean love is distant,
love is invisible?
Does that mean
we can be atheists
about love or at least
agnostic?
Or maybe it means
that love is not God.
Instead God is someone
who loves us in a way
that is definitional,
that is exemplary,
that can be discovered
in the most unexpected
places and that sometimes
a leaf falls at the exact right moment
and makes us think about
how perfect the whole world
is or could be and how
maybe
just maybe
I am loved
by someone
who knows
everything.

26

MYSTICAL LOVE

From matter's largest sphere,
we now have reached the heaven of pure light,
light of the intellect, light filled with love,
love of true good, love filled with happiness,
a happiness surpassing every sweetness.

DANTE ALIGHIERI

When I was a kid, I was told that if someone didn't believe in God—which meant not only the God of my religion but the very specific understanding of God in my subset of a subset of that religion—then that person couldn't be loving because "God is love."

In fact (and I'm embarrassed to say this), I left my Christian high school and entered college with the misconception that I was entering this world of people who (through no fault of their own) were not able to love each other. I hadn't really stopped to think about the implications: how this would mean that parents didn't love their children, that friendships would be loveless, that spouses would be in some sort of dreary life agreement. I didn't even think about the fact that I had friends who were both loving and not part of my religious circle.

It's tempting not to talk about "divine love" because we all have so many pictures of what this means, so many competing beliefs, so many arguments about theology. It even feels like we could wade into this and come out experiencing less love: hate and frustration with one another.

So let me be very clear here: I have strong feelings about who God is and what it means that God is loving. I also am pleased to report that people who disagree with me can and do experience love, both as people who love others and people who receive love. And yes, my atheist, agnostic, and other nontheistic friends also generate and receive love.

We could get into a big theological and philosophical conversation about what exactly is meant by divine love and how accessible it is to each person, but what I really want to get at is this: I believe that there is such a thing as ultimately perfect love in the world. I have not experienced that love from other human beings, though I have been lavished with human love to an extent that is well above the average. And yet, I believe I have experienced this divine love.

Divine love knows us fully and completely and still loves us without reservation or hesitation. It is love that exists without needing the power of our belief, love that persists without needing us to change, to apologize, to become better, or to make promises about the future. It doesn't need to control us. And although it doesn't need us to change, it does see the places where change in our lives would bring us greater happiness and fulfillment and would cause less damage to the people around us. This love desires change for our own, better lives—but is not dependent on that change.

Do you believe that love like this exists? For me as a Christian, I see love as a person, in the moment that God took on human form as Jesus, to bring human beings into deeper relationship with God. Maybe you struggle to think of divine love as a person at all . . . maybe you see it as a force, not even a "being" as such. Maybe for you, it's just a nice intellectual exercise, or maybe you're skeptical such a thing exists at all.

To which I can only say this: Divine love (the love of God) is ultimately mystical love. And mysticism is, by definition, about a personal experience. Of course, we won't believe in divine love if we haven't experienced it. But if we do experience it, it's natural to compare the perfect love of God with the love we have given to or received from others. We want our love and the love of those around us to match the pure love of the divine.

In that sense, one of the most beautiful things about divine love is its ability to transform our own love into something greater.

REFLECTION

Have you experienced love from God? Do you believe that God is love? Or do you struggle to believe that one or both of these things exist? Take a few moments to reflect on where you are on the question of divine love.

EXERCISE

This is an easy one today, though it might sound hard. I'm just going to ask you to be open to experiencing divine love. Get in a quiet place, alone, for just a few minutes. Take a deep breath and give your full attention to what you are doing. And then say these words, which you can think of as prayer or meditation or well wishes. But remember, we are seeking to connect with divine love. Just say this: "Please show me your love today." After you say those words, go about the rest of your day normally, paying attention to where the love of God might show up.

27

SERVICE

Love yourself. Then forget it. Then, love the world.
MARY OLIVER

For years I was on staff with a nonprofit, and every two years, we held a giant conference that all our staff—about five thousand people—went to. We all traveled to a central location, most people brought their families, and we spent a week and a half learning together, connecting with each other, singing, watching bands or comedians. It was a huge, fun thing, and I had been part of planning it for several years.

Including the summer that Shasta would ultimately pass away.

I was supposed to show up at the conference planning early in June, and the conference was mid-July. Shasta's health was failing, though we didn't realize how quickly it would happen, and her mom had moved in with her to help

111

on a daily basis. My own family was going through a little health crisis, too, and I was exhausted. Just worn through.

But I was helping lead this conference. People were depending on me. I was making plans to drive out and get our apartment all set up for when Krista and the kids arrived.

My coworkers (not just coworkers, but also friends, of course) kept asking me if that was really the best thing. One in particular, our friend Kourtney, kept calling and saying, "Are you sure you should be driving out?" I explained that I needed my car, this seemed like the best choice, and so on.

Kourtney finally convinced me to come late. To fly instead of drive. Helped me get a rental car. And when I arrived at the conference, she and another friend had completely set up our apartment already—bought food, made the beds, got all the pots and pans cleaned and put away. They even did things I would have never done, like buy decorative pillows.

My whole team, including my boss, my coleaders, and the people I reported to, were so generous and gracious to me that whole summer. They kept checking in on me. Sharing their own stories. Being patient while I was crying while leading a staff meeting, waiting for me to catch my breath so we could get back to work.

And I just felt . . . so overwhelmed and weird about being cared for in this way. I felt vulnerable and exposed. And I felt deeply, deeply cared for. Loved. People were choosing to do something for me—even things I claimed I didn't need, that I could do myself—because they were loving people who cared about me and my family and Shasta.

I've put this story here, in the "divine love" section, because every single one of those people would say they were living out something they had been taught by God. That God does things for them when they are in need, serves them when by all rights their job should be serving God.

In my faith tradition, we often tell a story of Jesus, just before he is about to die, doing something unexpected for his followers. He washes their feet. Some churches still do this today. In ancient times, washing feet was the servant's job, but when no servants were around, Jesus put a towel around his waist and got on his knees and washed the dirt and dust from his own followers' feet. When someone tried to get out of being served, Jesus told him that wasn't an option. And when he was done, he told them that if he, their leader, could serve them, they should serve each other.

It's amazing how often the reality of love comes back to this question: What can I do for you?

How can I take care of you?

What are your needs, and how can I help meet them?

REFLECTION

What needs do you see in the lives of people around you? How could you serve those people? What offers have others made—even small offers—to help take care of you? Have you said yes or no to those offers, and why?

EXERCISE

Do something for someone else this week. If you need
help thinking of a specific idea, consider these three
categories: (1) Is there a favor I can do for someone? (2)
Is there a way I can spend some money to help someone else? (3) Is there some physical labor I am able to
do that would benefit someone else?

28

FREEDOM TO LOVE

Let this presence settle into your bones, and allow your
soul the freedom to sing, dance, praise, and love.

TERESA OF ÁVILA

There were these kids in my grade school whom no one was supposed to love. Maybe you had them at your school too. What's sad, looking back, is that I was at a religious school. You would think that when the whole core of our curriculum was built around the idea of "love one another". . . maybe, just maybe, someone would have been on the lookout for this. Someone would have done something.

It didn't seem to matter where I went to school, though. Everyone knew which kids you weren't supposed to love. Maybe they looked funny, or smelled weird, or had some embarrassing moment in class. Sometimes it was because of something that had happened to them, like maybe their tragedy was contagious: lost a parent, burned in a fire, some sort of sickness. Sometimes it was because of the way the kid acted, things they did or said.

No one ever said, "Don't love those kids," but there was social pressure to back off. If you hung out with those kids, you were done with the group. Instead of bringing the outsider in, you'd be letting yourself out. "You're friends with *him*?" or "What, do you like her or something?" were common cues that you were in social danger because of whom you were hanging out with.

Even though I'm an adult now, this dynamic hasn't changed. I have been told not to love people because of their political party, their religion, their status as immigrants, their race or ethnicity, their sexual orientation or their gender. Sometimes people say this subtly, and sometimes they just say it outright. I'm guessing you've experienced this too.

And let's be honest, there are some people who are harder to love than others. People who are cruel, or who treat us poorly. People who make it clear they are our enemies, or that they hate people we love.

This is why divine love is important. In the Christian faith—when Christians haven't messed it up with their own inability to love and be loved—we are told that God's love is big enough for all of humanity. In fact, one of the most famous Bible verses—famous enough to be held up at baseball games—is John 3:16, which says that God loved the world so much that he sent Jesus.

The enormity of that love gives me considerable freedom.

If God, the divine being, loves all human beings, then there is no one "off-limits" for me to show love toward. And, also, if there are certain individuals whom I find myself unable to love because of our history, or because of my own issues, I can still be certain that they are loved. Not by me, but by God.

And it also means that as I make more room in my life for the divine presence—more room for God—I will become more loving, not less. When I see someone who is unkind and selfish, cruel, angry, a liar—the opposite of all the things about love we've been discussing—then I know that person is far from God and the divine love God's presence brings. And when I see those things in myself, then I know I am far from God. The surest sign of the presence of God in a life is the presence of deep love.

Yes, I have atheist friends who are deeply loving, and religious friends who are not. You might think that's an argument against my point, but I don't think it is. Some atheists are closer to God than some people who claim God, that's all.

And my job, your job, our job . . . is to love them both.

REFLECTION

What do you think of the idea that nearness to a loving God creates more love in the lives of human beings? Do you agree or disagree? Do you find the thought unsettling or comforting?

EXERCISE

Make a list of five people you have been told you shouldn't love—whether a grade-school friend, someone in your life, a politician, an actor, whomever. Is there something they all have in common? Are there good reasons for you to keep your distance (in other words, are people who love you telling you to keep distance because they care about you)? Next time someone implies that you can't or shouldn't love someone, just ask them straight-out: Why is this person not someone I should love?

29

IMAGINATION

Love is largely an act of imagination.
AMBER NICOLE BROOKS

*T*here's a well-known children's book about two rabbits—parent and child—trying to describe how much they love each other. Each time the child comes up with a way to share his love ("I love you as high as I can hop!"), the parent doubles the stakes ("But I love you as high as *I* can hop!"). It all culminates with the sleepy child saying, "I love you right up to the moon" and falling asleep before the parent whispers, "I love you right up to the moon—and back."[1]

And while in real life, that sort of interaction might get annoying eventually—a girlfriend and I went back and forth like this to the point of mutual frustration at being "one-upped" by the other—it points us to a core truth about how we learn love. Our love can only grow to the size we provide it, and there are two ways we create that space: what we have learned and believe about love, and what we imagine could be true about love.

As I've mentioned, I grew up with a significant advantage: extremely loving parents. So my expectations of what love should look like are pretty expansive. I expect love to include kindness, forgiveness, freedom, vulnerability, and so on. If someone grew up with a different type of relationship with those who raised them, their expectations might be different. Our expectations of what love looks like are formed by what we experience from our family, former and current relationships, and even the media—movies or books or podcasts that tell us what love is like.

Imagination, though, makes more room for love by asking, *Is there a way this could be better?* or *Could love be something more?*

I'm not talking about being unthankful ("I am unhappy—could I get something more than this?"), but rather suggesting that imagination gives us a greater, more expansive idea of *what is possible* with love. As our loving imagination expands, it creates more room for love to grow.

So, for instance, I might look at a loved one and think, *How could I make things even better for them?* Maybe I could be kinder when they ask a question I've answered a hundred times. Maybe I could make them a meal or express my love for them more clearly. It could be a small thing or a huge thing. All based in that key question: *Is there a way to make my love for them clearer, stronger, better?*

What can I imagine love to look like in this relationship? What things can I change to bring my love closer to that imagined reality?

What in this is divine love, you might wonder? Well, the loving, divine presence immerses us in a love that is deeper than we can find in human relationships. There is a purity, a fullness to the divine love that increases our imagination and our capacity to love.

For instance, if God loves me and also knows literally everything about me, then that teaches me to imagine a love where even the worst thing I have done does not mean I am unworthy of love. If God loves me enough to forgive me no matter the wrongs I commit, I learn to see the power of forgiveness and have the courage to offer it myself. If God's person defines love, that means as I grow and understand the divine nature better, I grow and understand love better.

And of course, Jesus had an expansive imagination when it came to love. He even says that a human being can live a completely moral life merely by being loving: Love God, and love other people.[2] Do those two things well, and you will never do something wrong.

What can you imagine love to be?

REFLECTION

Think about the most loving relationship you personally have observed. What were the hallmarks of it? Now: Can you imagine a relationship even better than that one?

EXERCISE
Get on your favorite social media and ask people to tell
you the most unbelievable love story they know. It can
be of any type—romantic love, love for a stranger, famil-
ial love—but look at the stories carefully. Which ones
seem unbelievable to you? Where does your imagination need to grow?

30

SACRIFICIAL LOVE

No one has greater love than this . . . to
be willing to die for a friend.[1]

ST. JOHN

I got the chicken pox in high school, and it was two weeks of horror. Everything itched. I was covered head to toe. I even had internal chicken pox, which meant that any food above lukewarm hurt to eat. My parents had to go to work, but in the late afternoon, my mom would go to the video store, get a giant pile of movies, and set them beside the TV for the next day. She focused on movies that were three hours long, so I'd get through the day faster and with minimum effort getting up. After work, she'd make milkshakes for me—one of the only things that felt good on my disgustingly raw throat—and make sure I had everything I needed.

In the middle of the night, I went to use the bathroom. I had a fever, and I felt woozy. One moment, I saw some pus coming out of one of my pox, and the next thing I knew, I woke up on the floor between the toilet and the shower and my dad was crouched beside me, rubbing my back. I had blacked out and hit the toilet and then the shower with my head, denting the door track.

I'm not a nurse or a doctor. I don't particularly want to take care of sick people. But most of us in deep relationship have had friends or family who have been sick. Parents, of course, are nearly certain to experience their share of mopping up puke and other unpleasant things because kids get sick and can't take care of themselves. I've held back my wife's (and my daughters', and my girlfriends', once upon a time) hair when she was throwing up (one memorable time when Krista had been eating strawberries, I thought she was dying because she started vomiting what looked like blood). I've held out bowls for people, have mopped up messes, and, yes, caught gross illnesses because I was taking care of my kids.

I wouldn't say I was happy to do those things. I don't know that my parents were happy to take care of me when I had chicken pox. We do these things that we don't really want to do because love is sacrificial. I do something I don't want to do—or don't do something I do want—because my beloved wants or needs something.

Of course, it's not just during times of sickness. It can be small things like the movie we choose to go to, the way we rearrange our time to let someone else do the thing they want, the color a bedroom is painted, the place we go on vacation, the direction the toilet paper is put on the roll. It can be huge things like voting for something that costs you but makes someone else's life better, or standing up for a coworker at the risk of your own job, or stepping between a child and a mountain lion.

Christians look at divine sacrificial love like this: God sent Jesus to humanity because God loved humanity. Jesus died—something he didn't want to do ("Take this cup from me," he prayed[2])—so that human beings could more fully experience divine love in their lives. God gives up power (by becoming human). God gives up life (by being killed). Why? Because the needs of human beings were important enough that the sacrifice was worth it.

That's sacrificial love . . . giving something up to benefit the person you love.

REFLECTION
When's a time someone gave something up because they loved you? When's a time you gave something up because of someone you love?

EXERCISE
Make a conscious choice this week to go against your own preferences so that you can give something to someone you love. It can be small, like choosing their favorite restaurant instead of yours. Or go big! Just remember that sacrificial love is a habit, not a one-time thing.

PART SEVEN

Love Changes the World

If I soaked a white cloth
in a bowl of dye
and it came out white
you'd say, "That's not dye."
If I soaked a red cloth
in a bowl of bleach
and it came out red
you'd say, "That's not bleach."
If I soaked my whole life
in a world of love
and it came out unchanged
you'd say, "That's not love."

31

LOVE AS ACTIVISM

Love is a revolution.
JON FOREMAN

 $\mathcal{W}$ hen I was in high school, my best friend Griz and I went to a local city-council meeting because it was—and I am not exaggerating—more entertaining than anything on television. There was a guy there who said that trees were more important than people. There was a man who called himself a "Jewish Nun" and did combination lecture/burlesque shows that were a satire of various religious traditions, all while wearing spectacular dresses and very high platform heels and a whole lot of makeup. And there was an extremely fundamentalist pastor who was running for council on a one-note moral platform.

All three of these people were what we might call "cartoon characters." They were so extreme in their positions that you couldn't believe you weren't watching a sitcom as the whole thing progressed. (I would watch this sitcom if you're listening, Hollywood.)

What I can't deny is that all three of these men had been catapulted into action because they loved something or someone. Tree Guy legitimately loved trees. Griz and I chatted with him after the meeting, and he gave us pins for his candidacy and got all teary-eyed talking about trees. And the gentleman nun (he identified as male) was legitimately protecting people whom he saw as being threatened by the fundamentalist pastor, who saw himself as protecting his people from moral decay.

Were they all right? I mean, no. Definitely not. But they were motivated, in some sense, by love . . . at least love for their own group, if nothing else. Love bleeds over into politics and the realities of our society. It can't help it. And that's because politics, seen through the eyes of love, are ultimately about people. Or at least that's the way it should be!

Love wants to change the world, and the reason love is so focused on this revolutionary ideal is that when we are loving the people around us, we see ways in which the world is not what it could be for people we love. We want it to be better. More accessible. More just. More loving.

This doesn't mean you have to run for office if you love people. But it should mean that our political decisions—in whatever government we live under—should be informed by our love for other people. And think "government" in the broadest sense: the people who are in charge. There are politics and "government" at our workplaces, our schools, our religious institutions, our clubs and sports teams and online hangouts.

Here's a small example of loving activism, in the context of middle school. My daughter Zoey attended a middle school under authoritarian leaders who were struggling to keep the school in line. They made strange rules and enforced them in odd and capricious ways. Parents lined up to talk to the principal and vice principal all the time, but it didn't seem to make any difference.

One strange thing was that there was a very specific dress code—one that was both more complex and also more strictly enforced for the girls. Even the parents weren't sure what to do. One parent told us, "I can't get shorts that are long enough for my daughter. Her legs are just too long." (The school would measure with tape from the knee to see if the shorts were long enough.) Punishments were overly harsh: privileges being revoked, including the end-of-year party run by the PTA (even though the PTA said they wanted all the kids to be there).

So one day a bunch of the guys at the school decided enough was enough. They all rolled up their shorts to be "too short" and made the teachers measure them. If they saw a girl getting measured, they'd swarm around and demand that they be measured too.

And the administration just sort of dropped it after that.

It's a silly example, but it gets to the heart of loving activism for me: The boys saw that the girls were being treated unfairly. Even though it didn't affect the boys, and even though it put them at risk to do so, they jumped in as activists to try to change it.

Love is risky, and active, and moves the world toward being a better place. If we're living in love, we're going to be a part of that.

REFLECTION

Love is political. And I know—we don't usually describe love or politics that way. When is the last time you saw clear, loving activism?

EXERCISE

Today's the day to do something. Write an email. Make a call. Make a statement. Take a stand. And wherever you do it, however you do it, try to do it in a way that shows love and respect to everyone, even those you disagree with.

32

COMPASSION

We are each made for goodness, love, and compassion. Our lives are transformed as much as the world is when we live with these truths.

DESMOND TUTU

$\mathcal{A}$ couple of years ago, I found a big piece of trash in my front yard. Or I thought it was trash, anyway. But when I looked closer, I discovered it was a "sky lantern"—a paper lantern that works like a hot-air balloon. You put a small flame under it, filling it with hot air, and it flies. Written on the lantern in Sharpie were the words, "I love you, Dad, I miss you so much. —Steph."

I had no idea who Steph was, but the words caught me off guard. Here was someone who had lost her dad and sent a loving message off into the world, probably never expecting a reply. I couldn't stop thinking about it all that day. I had already recycled the lantern, but it kept coming to mind. I kept thinking—if I died, and my three daughters sent a message like that, I'd want someone to respond to them. I didn't have any way to get ahold of Steph, but I knew I wanted to send a note to her somehow. So that night, late, after Krista and the kids went to bed, I stayed up and wrote a letter to Steph and posted it on my website.

The moment I pressed "post," I felt better, even though I knew the likelihood that Steph would ever see it was small.

We need to pause the story here, because what we're reflecting on today is compassion. That moment when I couldn't stop thinking about Steph and her hurt, that's compassion. It's this feeling when you see someone else hurting—an unease in your gut that you can't get rid of. Compassion is love's call to action.

And of course, compassion changes the world. Because when we see someone hurting, someone in need, someone in pain, compassion asks, *How do we fix that?* Many of the world's most powerful and important nonprofit organizations came from some story where their founder saw one person or one group of people in need and said, *I'm not going to rest until we've taken care of this.* Sometimes it's something small, like writing a letter or sending a text, and that changes the world too.

It might be that you don't feel compassion for others often. Usually—and I say this from experience—the places or topics where I don't experience compassion are ones where my own compassionate response has gone stagnant. The best way to awaken it is to acknowledge the times in the past when, instead of doing something when I felt compassion (and thus making myself and the person feel better), I hardened my heart by saying something like, "There's nothing I can do about that" (and thus made myself feel nothing).

By the way, Steph did see my letter! I mostly wrote about how much I knew her dad loved her, and was proud of her, and wanted good things for her life. Steph saw it somehow and reached out, and we became good friends. She's been out to visit with my family, and I've met her boys. She took my daughter Allie to the movies a while back when Allie was living near her. Steph also encouraged me to write some loving letters to my own daughters, which is pretty cool. Compassion moves us to action, and so often that action moves others to compassion.

And more often than not, that compassion creates a stronger, more loving community around us.

REFLECTION

When you get that feeling of compassion, are you more likely to do something or shut it down? Why is that? When's the last time you acted on compassion? When's the last time you didn't act on it?

EXERCISE

Next time you see someone getting dragged on social media or in the news, reach out to them and remind them that they are a human being who is worthy of love. If you feel comfortable, tell them you're available if they need to talk about something.

33

LOVE AND JUSTICE

Power at its best is love implementing the demands of justice, and justice at its best is power correcting everything that stands against love.

MARTIN LUTHER KING JR.

When I was in junior college, I met this man who was about the same age as my dad. We were in class one day, and the Vietnam War came up—my dad served in the Navy during that war—and this man in my class started sobbing. Just sobbing and sobbing, to the point that class couldn't go on. The teacher invited him to leave, but he couldn't. He said he needed to talk to us . . . to us, all these young college kids, most of us still teenagers.

"When I was in Vietnam," he said, "we had gone into this village. And you have to understand the kids . . ." He was saying all this between sobs. "The kids would come up and you would think they had food, but they would have a gun. They would kill you." He started to tell us all about how they went into this village, and they were scared. Someone began shooting at them from somewhere, and he and his fellow soldiers started firing into the village. The whole thing was jumbled. I wasn't sure if it was clear to him, even. But I remember so clearly the end of the story. It ended with him holding a Vietnamese boy who was dying from his injuries. "He was dying," he kept saying. "He had maybe four, five hours to go, and he was in terrible pain." He said he knew the kid was going to suffer. "So I took my hands, and I put them over his face, and I smothered him." The whole class sat in shocked silence. He looked at us, still sobbing, and asked, "Did I do the right thing? Do you think I did the right thing?"

I don't remember what any of us said. But I do remember after class, when we were all talking with one another, trying to figure out what we should have said. The irony wasn't lost on us that he was asking us, people in our late teens and early twenties—the same age he made his decision. We felt in over our heads, unsure and disagreeing about what we would have done. He had made his decision in that moment and was still agonizing over it all these years later.

Loving other people is the ultimate moral compass. If we love other people, and do it well, every other moral act hangs from that first rule of love.

It's still complicated, of course, and in this particular situation, we can get into all sorts of questions about war. When is it just? Should Americans have been in Vietnam? And on and on, backward into who made decisions that allowed an American teen and a Vietnamese boy to try to kill each other.

These things all come down to a question of justice—of right behavior that treats all people as they should be treated. Justice cannot be accomplished without love, because a lack of love is inherently unjust. Love is the engine of justice. People deserve to be treated justly because love demands it.

For instance, a young man was shot to death by police in my town earlier this month. We were told it happened during a drug bust. He tried to run and was killed. There are a lot of complicated ways we can approach the question of whether justice was done. Maybe we want more details: What kind of drugs? Was he carrying a firearm? Did any of the police officers know him? Why did he run? Was he scared? And while any of those details might help us—he was twenty-one, allegedly selling a few pills of prescription Xanax, he made a call to his girlfriend telling her that he was panicking while the police were searching for him—the most important question might be one of love.

What if you knew this kid? What if he took your neighbor's daughter to prom a few years ago, and you met him? What if you'd become friends, and you knew him to be a respectful kid? You knew he'd been struggling to make ends meet. He and his girlfriend had an infant son at home. Would that change the way that you'd understand justice in this situation? Was this kid's life worth a handful of Xanax?

It might be that your head is fighting against this narrative even now . . . that you're saying, "Well, he should have—" or "If he hadn't—" but the question is, if that kid were *someone you loved*, would the death penalty—no trial, no jail time, no lawyers—feel like a just outcome to you?

Almost certainly not.

It's hard, sometimes, to look through the lens of love to discover justice.

And yet, many of the most difficult issues of our day become much clearer through that lens . . . if we can find the strength to look through it.

REFLECTION

What are the three biggest justice issues in the world today? What would it look like to try to change those issues using love to guide both our decisions and our actions?

EXERCISE

There's something that's not right in the world around you. You know what it is—the thing that bothers you, that comes up so often and you try to ignore it. Do you need to write a letter? Make a phone call? Set up an appointment? Do you need to right an old wrong? Do you need to share a secret you've kept far too long? Here's permission to do something about it. Take a deep breath, be strong, be brave, and get to it.

34

LOVE AND THE TRANSFORMED HEART

Love transforms one into what one loves.

CATHERINE OF SIENA

$\mathcal{W}$hen Shasta was around, I was a more thankful person. She had a way of seeing the silver lining in a storm cloud and not only acknowledging it but celebrating it. Being thankful for it. The more I loved Shasta, the more I saw the world a different way. She said she had never seen an ugly person, a thought that was new to me. She wasn't joking, either. Every person she met was beautiful in some way.

Loving Krista has made me see the world more clearly. She loves people from other cultures in a way that was new to me when I met her. Krista has taught me to have more clarity about what I want in the world, and to be able to go after my dreams, when in the past I was content to daydream. She's also taught me about faithfulness and always doing what you promise.

My parents have taught me so much about love, I doubt I could lay it all out. Loyalty to family, generosity to others, kindness to strangers, how to build a loving community, how sometimes you can show love to someone in your words and other times through your actions or just by being there. They moved states just to be near my family. My sisters have taught me about commitment to the long haul, about forgiveness, about longevity in permanent relationships.

My kids teach me new things every day and shape who I am. Zoey teaches me about the importance of being focused on things that are meaningful to you and how to be satisfied with a few deep friendships instead of trying to build a thousand shallow ones. Allie teaches me about being aware of people around you and building relationships that are transformative beyond your circle of friends. Myca teaches me about the importance of being really confident in who you are and that it doesn't matter what others think, and also about the beauty of deep compassion.

JR. has taught me a lot about justice and about taking care of myself. His wife, Amanda, helps me to be more warm and hospitable. Clay has a way of making every person he talks to feel like the center of the universe. His wife, Jen, maximizes the strengths of everyone around her.

Clay and JR. started our podcast, and we reached out to a woman named Kathy Khang, who has joined us too. She's become like a sister and teaches me a lot about speaking up and not trying to sound like an ambassador all the time when I'm sharing my opinion.

Then there are my in-laws, my brother and sister-in-law and nephew, and many other friends who are deeply a part of my life, like my old friend Latifah, the Chens, the Smiths,

Ken and Sarah, and a family called the Reeves who are far more than friends to us.

It's an embarrassment of riches when I start to think about all the people I would want to name here and the ways they've made my life better. The point is this: My life isn't just better because they love me. My life is better because by loving them, I am becoming more like them. They give me insights into myself and the world around me that allow me to be changed, to be transformed, and I become a better person.

It sounds ridiculous, but if you want to grow as a human being, find a person you want to be more like and do your best to be a good friend to them. And good friends—our best friends, those who love us most and we love in return—end up leaving marks on us that can't be taken away. We become a part of them, and they become a part of us.

No matter what comes, love has changed us.

REFLECTION

Think of one significant relationship in your life that started at a point you remember. Maybe you met at work or in the first grade. What was your life like before you met? And how have you changed as a person since then?

EXERCISE

Make a list of the people you love in life. How have they changed you for the better? For extra credit, send them a little note and tell them about it.

35

LOVE FOR STRANGERS

The hardest spiritual work in the world is to love the
neighbor as the self—to encounter another human being
not as someone you can use, change, fix, help, save, enroll,
convince or control, but simply as someone who can spring
you from the prison of yourself, if you will allow it.

BARBARA BROWN TAYLOR

On social media tonight, I came across a video of these five friends. Five men who clearly love one another and have a great time together. I can tell they have each other's backs. They were doing a sort of video podcast and talking about their industry—one that I'm connected to and have some friends in—and then they started talking about this woman whom they really dislike. A woman who has cancer, and whom I consider one of my friends, though we've never met face-to-face. And then they started in with the "jokes." Jokes about cancer. Jokes about my friend.

They said that God had given her cancer because she had crossed them in some way in their industry. They said she deserved it. They cursed at her and spat her name like it was a curse itself. And I know this woman. I know she is not some monster. She is kind. She loves people around her. She and I have written back and forth, and she's told me things about her partner and her family, and I've done the same.

These five men failed to love her. She's not a part of their group—they have different politics and theologies, different ideas of what the world should look like—and so they celebrated her having cancer. Which . . . having walked through it with Shasta, I cannot imagine celebrating cancer in any human being, no matter how much I disliked them.

I noticed something important as I studied my own reaction to these five men.

I wanted to do the same thing to them. Not laugh about their cancer, should they get it, but I definitely wanted to write them off, remove them from the category of "human," and put them instead in some subhuman place that would allow me to treat them with hatred, contempt, anger, impatience, cruelty.

I'll not pretend that my responsibility to them is the same as my responsibility to my friend. Of course it is not. She needs to be supported and held up. Protected, stood up for, checked in with. And the most loving things those men need right now might not feel loving to them: honesty, clarity, critique, a description of what should be and where they are and the vast difference between those two places. The most loving thing that can be done for them is to show them how badly they have messed up.

But I have to acknowledge that my instinct is to treat them

the same way they treated my friend. I am not better than they are. I am the same. Worse, what's harder for me in this moment to embrace is this: Those five men are worthy of love right now, without changing or becoming better, without being fixed or convinced or controlled. As horrible as their words and actions toward my friend are, they are still worthy of love. Maybe I'm not the one who will be able to do it. Maybe it won't be my friend who does it. But they are human beings. They are "my neighbors," and they should be loved.

My heart screams against that. Fights it, rails against it.

Sometimes in the journey to love, we don't know the next step. We don't know the way from here to where we want to be. And I've discovered through bitter experience that sometimes I can find the way forward by searching my heart for the people—the strangers—I find hardest to love. That reveals a place I haven't allowed love to transform me. That reveals a space I can grow into, can let love change. It's a reminder that I'm still on the journey, and an invitation to keep climbing. For a loving person, there can be no strangers . . . only beloved human beings we have yet to meet.

REFLECTION

I've been on both sides of this. I've been the uncaring person who refuses to love the people around me. I've also been the victim, the person whom someone has treated poorly and refused to love. How about you? How long ago was the experience? What was it like?

145

EXERCISE

It's easy to love people who love us. Think about someone you just find really difficult. (This should be someone you don't know well and aren't already in deep
relationship with.) Maybe this person is opposite from
you politically or spiritually or philosophically. What
would it look like for you to love this person well?

PART EIGHT

Strength to Love

Do you have the strength to climb this mountain?
You cannot say when you are standing at the base.
You may have harnesses and helmets
Socks and slings, Camalots and carabiners,
But intention never guarantees ascension.
No, it is when you are standing near the summit,
The thin air white when you breathe it out,
Your chest tight, your legs numb with cold and
Your friend says, "Are you ready?"
Clouds roll by below, the valley blue in the distance.
It's not that it's never been done before.
It's not that you've never been there.
But how badly do you want it?
Do you feel a holy dissatisfaction
with the ground beneath your feet?
Do you want to go higher?

36

REST IN LOVE

Love turns work into rest.
TERESA OF ÁVILA

*E*ventually on the journey to love, we all reach the same fear: *Do I have the strength for this? Can I really love someone the way that true love requires?*

Love is a lot like riding a bicycle through hill country. Some moments are intensely painful and you're not sure you can turn the pedal one more time, and then, suddenly, the wind is in your face and it feels like it takes nothing to move that bike, and you feel like you could do this forever. The two, of course, are related. Whether you start at the top of the hill or the bottom, eventually you come to the opposite place. You won't experience the easy free fall of love without the hard work to get to the summit, and you won't feel the burn of the hard work if you've only ever ridden on flat ground.

Many of the aspects of love we've already discussed give us strength in the hard times. Patience, knowing that this time of hard work will pass eventually. Perseverance, the ability to keep going. Hope, the knowledge that better things will come in time. Selflessness, the assurance that if this is the best thing for those you love, you can take a little hard work to get there.

But there is a strange reality that comes in our most loving relationships. The work—even the toil to pedal up the mountain—sometimes feels like nothing. Love can, as Teresa of Ávila said, turn work into rest. Sometimes the work of love feels enjoyable, fun, fulfilling, even restful. At the end of the day, you aren't exhausted but thankful somehow for the hard work you have put in.

If you are in the midst of the hard uphill climb, I'd encourage you with this: It's okay to take a break for a while too. Love doesn't disappear overnight. I can get so wrapped up in trying to fix things and working hard that I forget the peace of remembering that if you love this person and they love you, too, it's okay for you to pause to regain your breath. They're not going anywhere, and neither are you, and sometimes time will move things along when brute force can't.

After Shasta died, I had many friends and family take care of me. Krista. My parents. My kids. Many of my friends called me, or texted, or just checked in. JR. started talking to me about "self-care" . . . something I didn't do much and needed to grow in. Sometimes the work of love is the work of allowing others to care for you when you are out of strength. Love can carry you when you're not able to go on.

And in the day-to-day experience of love, something that might be work in another context feels like nothing at all. I don't enjoy cleaning the kitchen, but when I do it because it makes Krista happy, it feels like less work than when "it just needs doing."

Which brings me to my last thought about the work of love for today. Sometimes the "work" is harder because I have forgotten why I am doing it. The exhaustion of caring for a sick loved one, the pain of waiting for a wayward loved one to return, the terrible agony of patience while waiting for someone we love to grow through some moment of awful transformation—all can be lessened by just reminding myself that embracing this exhaustion, accepting this pain, and acknowledging the need for patience is, in and of itself, an act of love.

REFLECTION

Who has worked hardest to love you well? Which relationships are you in where love seems to come effortlessly? Which ones are a struggle? Why do you think that is?

EXERCISE

No exercise today . . . just relax in the reality of the love of others for you and the love you have for others.

37

THANKFULNESS

When you arise in the morning, think of what a precious privilege
it is to be alive—to breathe, to think, to enjoy, to love.

MARCUS AURELIUS

One day when I was driving Shasta to her chemotherapy appointment, she asked me to stop the car in the middle of the road. There were trees blooming overhead, making a canopy over the street, and she wanted to stop and smell the flowers. She got up, put her face through the sunroof, and breathed it in. "I'm so thankful the trees are blooming," she said.

She had this generous thankfulness that continued to the end of her life. She told me often how thankful she was for me, for various friends, for her parents and family, for the condo she lived in, for her dog, for things that had happened in the past or things she came across in the moment.

The more time I spent with her, the more thankful I became too. Thankfulness helped me see the world in a new and different way. In my closest relationships, I was quicker to focus on the many wonderful things about my loved ones. I more readily experienced thoughts of kindness toward those around me. Thankfulness skewed the world toward loveliness.

One thing I feared after Shasta died was that I would lose the sense of wonder that comes from being thankful for the world around me. So I tried out a new habit for a time. At the beginning of each week, I did a social-media post of things I was thankful for.

When we are out of the habit of thankfulness, it's easy to think, *I have nothing to be thankful for.* This can feel particularly true in difficult seasons. When I set out to start this practice, I was in a deep well of personal grief. But thankfulness helped me to see things a different way.

What I learned was this: There is always something to be thankful for because the world is full of good things. On even my worst day, I could at least say, "I am thankful for the air I breathe." I could be thankful for my health. My family. The beauty of the natural world. The fact that I had the luxury of time to stop and make a social-media post. Friends. I could even be thankful—if I was struggling in the moment—for things or people or events of my past.

But what does thankfulness have to do with love?

Thankfulness makes us more aware of the presence of love. It increases our feelings of affection for those who are already in our lives. It reminds us of the many good things about difficult people we know. It reorients us toward recognizing blessings rather than focusing on problems. It gives us more space to pause and create time for others . . . because we come to expect good things from interactions with other people.

Also—and this shouldn't have surprised me, but it did— my thankfulness creates more thankfulness in the people around me. I experienced this from hanging out with Shasta, but I didn't expect it would be the case with me. As I shared my own thankful thoughts more vocally, the people around me did too. More people told me what they were thankful for and expanded my vision for things to be thankful for in the world. And, shockingly, more people took time to thank me for things about me.

Thankfulness is contagious. And it increases our capacity for love.

REFLECTION
Do you find it easy or difficult to be thankful? Does it come to you naturally, or do you have to work at it?

EXERCISE
Every day, make a mental list of five things you are thankful for. For extra credit, share those five things with someone. If you can't think of five new things every day, you can even have a list of things that are always true to be thankful for, and just revisit them daily (air to breathe, a loved one, coffee). You may be surprised to discover that being thankful for the same things every day eventually causes you to recognize new things you are thankful for!

38

FAITHFULNESS

I believe that I am very lucky to have close friends who are faithful.
JULIA CAMERON

𝒜 counselor visited a group of men I was a part of and wanted us all to share our "father wounds." By which he meant those tragic interactions with our fathers that have shaped us and created toxic and destructive behavior in our own lives. As my friends shared various things—some horrible, some relatively mild—I felt a sort of dread. I couldn't think of one. Not that my dad never made a mistake, but did he do something so damaging that I had an unhealed wound decades later? No. I said as much, and the counselor gave me a condescending look and said, "It's okay if you don't feel comfortable sharing."

My parents are the definition of faithfulness. I've learned as I've gotten older that this is not the most common reality, and it's a real gift that my loving parents gave me. They never hit me when they were angry, they didn't purposely say cruel things to me, they were always available when I had trouble, and they loved to help me with whatever issue was in front of me. They were supportive, kind, encouraging, and vocal about their love for me. I legitimately have nothing to complain about beyond the most minor and common relational problems (we annoy one another sometimes).

Faithfulness is this idea that whatever comes, someone will still be there. It's more than perseverance—someone who is faithful is someone you can't imagine disappearing. You can predict what their response will be to this problem or that: They will be in your corner. Which means if you mess up, they will tell you so—but they will also tell you they still love you. Forgiveness is a given. Faithfulness is the guarantee of presence, the certainty of permanent relationship.

So, for example, when I was in middle school and my best friend and I took my BB gun, set up G.I. Joe action figures all over the house, and shot at them, blowing holes in a giant window and also a globe chandelier, did I lie when my parents found out? *Of course* I lied. I blamed my buddy for everything. Was I worried that I would be hurt, physically or emotionally? Kicked out of the family? Given a bloody nose? No. None of that ever occurred to me.

I realize that may be hard to wrap your mind around if you've not had faithfulness modeled in your life somewhere. So let me tell you this: Faithfulness is possible. You can stay faithful even if someone else walks away from a relationship.

Sometimes that might mean something as simple as wishing them the best in their life without you.

Faithfulness means that, at the end of the day, you are committed to what is best for someone. That can mean a lot of different things, and it doesn't always mean capitulating to what they want. (I sure didn't want to have my BB gun taken away, but, well, I clearly couldn't be trusted with it.)

Faithfulness give us strength to love because it's a mental decision that we make at some point in our relationship: *I'm not going anywhere, whatever comes.* It removes the constant back-and-forth of *Should I be available?*[†] When I am faithful, it becomes ludicrous to even ask the question. If someone told me, "Your parents have said they don't want to be in relationship with you," I would know that to be a lie. Angry? Maybe. Not want to be in relationship with me? Never.

This may be one of the more difficult attributes of love to understand if you haven't experienced it. If you've never seen faithfulness, the entire way you see the world emerges from the belief that there is no such thing as someone who is faithful, no relationship that is not, on some level, people using each other until the relationship fails to fulfill them anymore. If that's your experience, I'd just ask this: Take a look around. Can you find a relationship—even a really exceptional, almost unbelievable one—where that isn't the

---

[†] An important caveat: Faithfulness doesn't mean you have to put up with cruel or abusive behavior from the person you love. Abusive or manipulative people might try to take advantage of our faithfulness . . . and that means they have walked away from your loving relationship already. It is wise, at that point, to break away from them. For more on this, see the note on abuse on page 167.

case? And if so . . . can you watch that relationship? Learn from it? Copy it? I believe you can find it. Not only that, I believe you can be in a relationship where faithfulness is a given. Don't settle for less than that.

REFLECTION

What are the boundaries of faithfulness for you? Who has been most faithful in your life? In whose life have you been most faithful? Are there "deal breakers" for you that cause you to say, "I can't show faithful love after something like that"?

EXERCISE

If you are coming from a place where faithfulness is rare in your life, start with something small. How about committing to reaching out to a specific loved one with encouraging words once a week for a year? That's fifty-two times. Too much? How about once every two weeks?

If you've been blessed with a faithful friend or loved one, take some time today to tell them how much you appreciate this part of your relationship. Call them, send them a text, or write them a letter.

39

SELF-CONTROL

Self-control might be as passionate and as
active as the surrender to passion.
WILLIAM SOMERSET MAUGHAM

"I'm so sorry. That wasn't like me!"

Have you ever heard an apology like that, or made one? It's usually followed by an explanation of why someone did the thing they did: I was tired. I was hungry. I've had a rough week.

In my religious tradition, sometimes people do long "fasts"—extended periods where we eat no food. I once did a lengthy (multiple-week) fast and discovered that I was cranky, irritable, and prone to getting angry at the people around me. It was tempting to say, "Well, if I weren't fasting, I would be more patient." I wanted to believe that my natural state was kinder, gentler, more loving than my weak-from-lack-of-food state.

But here's the truth: Anything I do is not only *like* me, it

But here's the truth: Anything I do is not only *like* me, it *is* me. If I did it, thought it, said it, that's because I am the type of person who would do, think, or say that thing in the situation I was in. Perhaps it was an extraordinary situation, yes, but still . . . that's what I would do in that situation. Saying "That's not like me" prevents me from looking honestly at who I am.

Self-control matters when it comes to love. If I am an angry person, I need self-control to prevent myself from harming those I love when I'm angry. If I am a fearful person, I need self-control to act with courage when love demands it.

Children (ours or other people's) often stretch us in this area. When one of my kids was a toddler, she went through a brief biting phase. One day I was walking past her in a hallway and she bit me—hard—right at her mouth level, which just happened to mean that she bit me in the crotch. My first instinct was to bring my fist down on her head because I was in so much pain. But I froze with my fist above my head and instead said (through gritted teeth) for her to stop biting. Which she did. Then there was a long, tearful lecture about not biting people. (I was the one crying. I was in a lot of pain.)

Self-control can be paired with many other attributes we've been talking about too. Self-control and patience can help you decide whether now or later is the best time to talk to someone about their character issues or behavior. Self-control and selflessness can give us the strength to work hard for the needs of other people, even when we find it painful. We cannot be gentle without self-control.

Two helpful tips in building self-control: First, we must know ourselves well. We have to identify where we're tempted to make excuses (such as "That's not like me") and remove them from our lives. I need to know the limits of my strengths, the realities of my weaknesses. Where am I most likely to lose control? Which things set me off? When do I need extra self-control or stronger boundaries in the relationships around me? This is true at home or at school, at work, in our neighborhoods, on the internet.

Second—and this is no small thing—is that we will have greater access to self-control when we are taking care of ourselves. It's not a coincidence that when I am tired or hungry or sick, I have a harder time with self-control. So as we are growing in this skill, we need to make sure that we are well rested, well fed with healthy food, getting what we need to deal with stress (exercise, space for quiet times, connection with good friends). Better self-care leads to better self-control.

I have this friend who has never yelled at his kids. Not once. I asked his kids, and they don't remember it ever happening. I don't yell often, but I don't have a track record like his. One time we were on a business trip together and before we got on the plane, he told me how tired he was. He just wanted to sleep. When we hit the tarmac at home, I saw him coming off the plane and he hugged this young, developmentally disabled kid. The kid's seat had been beside

161

my friend's. It was this kid's first time flying, and he was scared. So my buddy—instead of sleeping—stayed up the whole flight, chatting with the kid and helping him have a good first ride on an airplane. That's the amazing way that love exhibits itself through self-control.

REFLECTION

When are you most likely to struggle with self-control? What sets you off? What might help you to grow in your ability to be self-controlled in the places that are hardest for you?

EXERCISE

Choose a single area of self-care that will help you grow in self-control (an earlier bedtime, a regular exercise time, a shift toward healthier food, a regular time with friends, etc.). Set a goal for change in that area, small or large. Then work to meet that goal. How does pursuing that goal affect your ability to exhibit self-control over time?

40

THE REMEDY FOR LOVE

There is no remedy for love but to love more.
HENRY DAVID THOREAU

*Y*ou cannot replace a love that is lost. Love can only be increased, not replaced. Whether the loss happens from broken relationship, death, or natural distance or time—the deeper that love, the greater the pain, and the more central this truth becomes.

In our pain, the temptation becomes to shut ourselves off to new love . . . whether new relationships or increased depth to old ones. After Shasta's death, I couldn't sleep for weeks. I still had many friends and loved ones, of course, and the ones closest to me were going through grief of some kind after Shasta's loss, as well. But my temptation, the thing I had to work through, was this desire to just be done with anything or anyone new. I was happy to stick with my wife, my kids, my family, and a few close friends.

Ironically, during this time of loss, many people were reaching out and offering deeper friendship, offering to process things, offering to walk through it all with us. But I didn't want to deepen my current relationships, either. I kept saying to myself, *That just wouldn't be the same.* Which is, it turns out, correct. It's not the same. But that doesn't mean it's bad, or even inferior. It's just different.

But the person who reminded me that we have to keep loving, keep opening ourselves to new relationships and new depths of relationship was, of course, Shasta herself. Or, that is to say, my memories of her. Not long before she passed, she invited one of the clerks from her local grocery store to come over for dinner with her and her mom. Over the years of her treatment, she became friends with one of the nurses who had often been with us—a nurse who still stays in touch with me today.

We often think of our capacity and need for love as a finite thing. That if we could just get a little more love in life, we would be satisfied—and if we got too much, we would be overwhelmed. But that doesn't happen! As you love more, as you accept more love, your capacity for love increases. It's like a muscle—the more you use love, the stronger it becomes.

In the pages of this book, we have been on a journey together, a journey toward greater love. Love is a journey without an end destination. Any time we think we have arrived, we discover another step, another path, another relationship in which to journey. That doesn't mean we can never be satisfied, or never reach a place of balance in our relationships—it just means that love, by its nature, always requests that we do more for our beloved ones. It just means that we, as objects of love, are always willing to receive more love.

As Thoreau said, the remedy to love is to love more. Even when we think its capacity is gone, love comes in unexpected and even miraculous ways.

In the last couple weeks of Shasta's life, my phone broke, and I took it in to the shop to be repaired while I used a loaner. As is often the case with such things, some texts got lost along the way. A couple days after she passed away, I went and got my old phone back and turned it on.

And I got a text . . . from Shasta.

It said, "I'm home now."

Yes, it was probably from a previous trip home from the hospital. Just a loving little note keeping me aware of where she was and what was going on.

But somehow, somehow—that text was waiting for me a couple days after she left us and moved on into the heavenly realms. I can't help but think that's a little miracle of love, set aside for me by God or Shasta or both.

Love is as strong as death. For even when death comes, love remains.

And in love we all—each and every one of us—find our home.

REFLECTION

How have you seen your love grow from the time
you started this book? Are you more aware of love?
Accepting more love? Giving more love away?

EXERCISE

The journey isn't over. What relationship do you need to
be more loving in? Where do you need to accept more
love from someone? Is there a new relationship you
need to create? Choose one of these places you want to
grow in love, and make a plan. You deserve to be loved,
and so do the people around you.

All you need is love.
But a little chocolate now and then doesn't hurt.
CHARLES SCHULZ

A NOTE ON ABUSE

*A*busers and manipulators take advantage of the vulnerability of loving people to control them and get their way. Love—real, actual love—includes these amazing, powerful things like forgiveness and letting go of past wrongs in a relationship. That's incredible. But it's important to remember that forgiveness looks different when you're dealing with abuse. An abuser takes forgiveness and uses it as a tool to get their way. They harm others and then say, "You're not forgiving" when they do it over and over, with no intent to change.

And just like we had to tell my friend Victoria "That's not love" when she described the abusive behavior of her husband, we need to look carefully at the relationships we're in and make sure that we're not endlessly pouring love into a relationship designed to hurt or damage us.

Some questions to ask:

1. Is this person consistently humiliating or embarrassing me?
   (Love doesn't shame people.)

2. Is this person frequently insulting or speaking cruelly to me?
   (Love is kind.)

3. Does this person betray our relationship?
   (Love is faithful.)

4. Does this person say things like "I love you, but . . ."
   (Love doesn't fail.)

5. Is this person demanding that I behave lovingly but not being loving themselves?
   (Love is selfless.)

6. Is this person trying to control me using money, withdrawal of affection, domination?
   (Love focuses on self-control. Not control of others.)

7. Is this person constantly possessive and suspicious of other relationships in my life?
   (Love is not possessive.)

Everyone messes up sometimes. But if this is a consistent pattern in your relationship with anyone—parent, spouse, partner, sibling, friend, lover, coworker—that's not love. You don't have to deal with that alone, and you don't have to stay in a relationship that is abusive. That's not loving to yourself . . . or to the person abusing you. They will not change so long as you stay in the relationship.

You deserve to be loved.

There are loving people out there.

Abusive people try to prevent you from finding loving relationships, but loving relationships are waiting for you.

Take courage. The journey to love is not for the faint of heart, but every step along the way gets easier. Love will find you.

ACKNOWLEDGMENTS

When I was first pitching this book, there were two friends and publishing professionals who sat down with me and told me (in the most loving way possible) that it wasn't working. The reason it wasn't working, they told me, was that I wasn't being honest. I wasn't being vulnerable. I wasn't allowing myself into the book. And, they said, I was avoiding hard feelings about Shasta's passing. They were absolutely right. I went home that night and wrote the current introduction, and that's how we ended up with *Journey to Love* in its current form . . . which was, by the way, much more difficult to write than what I had planned. Those two people were Don Pape and Caitlyn Carlson. I can honestly say this book wouldn't exist without both of their insights, encouragement, and feedback along the way, and I am profoundly grateful.

I am deeply thankful to so many people for their impact on my life and this book: Mom and Dad, of course; my sisters, Lynn and Dawn, and my brother-in-law Todd; Janet and Terry; Kevin, Shimmra, and Jonas; JR. and Amanda;

Kathy and Peter; Clay and Jen; Elliott and Lauren; Aaron; and Latifah, who is often my companion when I am growing and learning about love. Special thanks to Kourtney Street and Glen Nielsen for letting me share stories about their loving presence, and to Griz, who I didn't even ask because if you go to the Concord City Council meetings, whatever happens there is fair game forever.

Huge thanks also to the whole NavPress team: Caitlyn Carlson (who deserves to be thanked more than twice, but hey, we gotta leave some room for everyone else), Elizabeth Schroll (copy editor extraordinaire), Olivia Eldredge, and David Zimmerman. These people are heroes. Books are a team effort, and I'm thankful for this team. A bunch of my buddies over at Tyndale snuck in here, too . . . Ron Kaufmann (who designed the incredible cover), Robin Bermel, Linda Schmitt, Whitney Harrison, and Danika King (*waves exuberantly*). Special thanks also to Cory Verner and the whole ONE Audio team for their hard work on the audio version.

I must always remember to thank my wise, kindhearted, loving friend Wes Yoder, who happens to be my agent but is, more importantly, a constant reminder of what a loving person looks like in the world.

Krista: You have taught and continue to teach me a great deal about love, and I'm thankful that we're such a good pair . . . strong where the other is weak, and learning from one another's best, most loving characteristics. I'm thankful for you. Looking forward to many more years together.

Myca, Allie, and Zoey: It's easy to love each of you. You're each so gifted, so wonderful, and just a pleasure to have in my life. I love you deeply and forever.

Bruce: You are a rabbit. But that doesn't mean you aren't worthy of love. Please stop biting through my computer power cords. Honestly, that's my one complaint.

To you, my readers, I leave this blessing: May the love you already have grow even greater. May the places where love is lacking be filled. Where there is hurt, find healing. Where there are tears, may you find comfort. May you continue to learn to accept more love and have the courage and strength to be more loving. You are worthy and deserving of love. May your journey to love be short and full of joy.

NOTES

1. LOVE EXISTS

1. 1 Corinthians 13:13.
2. For more on this topic, see Aatish Bhatia, "The Crayola-fication of the World: How We Gave Colors Names, and It Messed with Our Brains (Parts I and II), *Empirical Zeal* (blog), June 5 and 11, 2012, empiricalzeal.com/2012/06/05/the-crayola-fication-of-the-world -how-we-gave-colors-names-and-it-messed-with-our-brains-part-i/; and empiricalzeal.com/2012/06/11/the-crayola-fication-of-the -world-how-we-gave-colors-names-and-it-messed-with-our-brains -part-ii/.
3. See, for example, Caleb Everett, "'Anumeric' People: When Languages Have No Words for Numbers," Live Science, April 30, 2017, livescience.com/58900-anumeric-people-with-no-words-for -numbers.html.
4. Shuruppak (sometimes spelled Shuruppag) shared this and other wisdom with his son in what is now called "The Instructions of Shuruppak." English translations of this Sumerian text are available free online.
5. Job 10:12, NRSV.

10. FORGIVENESS

1. Matthew 18:21-22, author's paraphrase.
2. Online Etymology Dictionary, s.v. "pardon (v.)," accessed January 8, 2021, etymonline.com/search?q=perdonare.

NOTES

13. LOVE IS NOT EASILY ANGERED
1. 1 Corinthians 13:5, NIV.

16. THE POWER OF TRUTH
1. Proverbs 27:6, WEB.

17. THE POWER OF HOPE
1. 1 Corinthians 13:7, NIV.

18. THE POWER OF COURAGE
1. 1 John 4:18, NKJV.

20. LOVE AND DEATH
1. Song of Solomon 8:6.

29. IMAGINATION
1. Sam McBratney and Anita Jeram, *Guess How Much I Love You* (Somerville, MA: Candlewick Press, 1994).
2. Matthew 22:36-40.

30. SACRIFICIAL LOVE
1. John 15:13, author's paraphrase.
2. Luke 22:42, NIV.